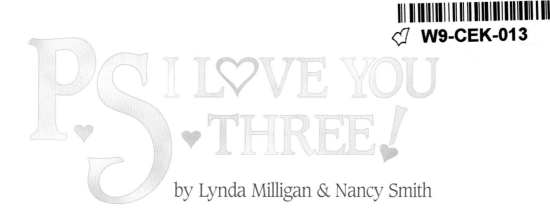

P.S. I LOVE YOU THREE!

by Lynda Milligan & Nancy Smith

Dedication

With deep love and appreciation we dedicate this book to our children.

They were the reason we made baby quilts in the first place—lasting treasures that would warm their bodies and nurture their souls. They have always believed in us and have supported us in so many ways. Their continued involvement in our business makes our success possible.

Richie Milligan – a fourteen-year-old who loves sports (and a girl now and then)

Kimberly Harbert – a junior at the University of Northern Colorado

Laura Smith – a senior at the University of Colorado

Rachel Smith – an independent film producer in Los Angeles, California

Ashley Smith Lawler – Director of Marketing Development and Human Resources at Great American Quilt Factory and Possibilities®

Jack Patrick Lawler – Ashley's one-year-old who comes to work with her every day

How lucky we are to be blessed with five beautiful children and one fantastic grandchild!

…Fabric Designers for AvLyn, Inc., publishers of DreamSpinners® patterns & I'll Teach Myself™ & Possibilities® books… Home of Great American Quilt Factory, Inc.

Special Thanks

Sewing – Susan Auskaps, Jane Dumler, Courtenay Hughes, Joanne Malone,
Ann Petersen, Nancy Smith, Katie Wells, Sue Williams

Machine quilting – Joanne Malone, Ann Petersen, Nancy Smith, Katie Wells

Long-arm machine quilting – Sandi Fruehling, Susan F. Geddes, Kay Morrison, Carolyn Schmitt

Furniture for photography – Guys & Dolls in Englewood, Colorado

Book Production

Sharon Holmes – Editor, Technical Illustrator

Susan Johnson – Designer, Graphics, Photo Stylist, Illustrator

Lexie Foster – Cover, Designer, Graphics, Photo Stylist, Illustrator

Christine Scott – Editorial Assistant

Sandi Fruehling – Copy Reader

Brad Bartholomew – Photographer

Together we produce great books of which we can all be proud.

...Fabric Designers for AvLyn, Inc., publishers of DreamSpinners®
patterns & I'll Teach Myself™ & Possibilities® books...
Home of Great American Quilt Factory, Inc.

P.S. I Love You Three!

©2002 Lynda Milligan & Nancy Smith

Published in the United States of America by Possibilities®, Denver, Colorado
Library of Congress Catalog Card Number: 2002103186
ISBN: 1-880972-47-6

Table of Contents

A bond of love conveyed through a quilt warms the heart and comforts the soul. The original, *P.S. I Love You*, was published in 1990, and *P.S. I Love You Two* followed in 1996. Now, six years later, another addition is made, *P.S. I Love You Three*. As our families have grown, so has our love of quilts. Fresh designs and new techniques have inspired us to create treasures of love for our new generation.

P.S. I Love You was written when our youngest, Lynda's son Richie, was still a baby. As we created quilts for the book, we reminisced about the quilts we had used in our own kids' nurseries and the other special quilts we had made for them over the years.

Now, in *P.S. I Love You Three* we find our children growing up and starting to have babies of their own. The cycle continues, and the generations forge ahead. Several of the quilts in the new book will be made in anticipation of new grandchildren. What a joy to have this opportunity. Security blankets never go out of style!

P.S. I Love You Three contains a wealth of projects that will encourage and inspire you to make many treasured heirlooms. It is a comprehensive book that features quilts for easy, intermediate, and complex skill levels. The colors range from soft, muted pastels to bright crayon colors. Each quilt sparks the imagination to make a one-of-a-kind nursery.

Complete and easy-to-understand yardage and cutting charts, directions, and diagrams are given for over 20 quilts in a variety of sizes: CRIB, CUDDLE, and TWIN. The cuddle size is great for older children to wrap themselves in to watch a movie or to place at the foot of their bed, handy for napping. Accessories compliment the quilts and include bumper pads, crib sheets, dust ruffles, wall hangings, sheets, pillows, baby boxers, hooded cuddlers, cold/hot pack cover, crib organizer, appliqued receiving blankets, and toys.

We never tire of making sweet and wonderful baby quilts. The ideas continue to flow, and the only major problem we ever have in writing a P.S. I Love You book is finding a way to stop before the book becomes the size of an encyclopedia!

Babies are the hope of tomorrow, and quilts are their comforters. P.S. I Love You says it all.

Ava Diggle and Aina Martin, our moms, and the "dignified elders" of four generations involved in our business. Ava helps out when she's in town, and Aina's job title is Accounts Payable and Payroll. 1988

Here we are, generation two, accepting the Jean Yancey Women in Business award. 1988

Ashley Smith and Kim Harbert, third generation, with us at the first Quilt Market we attended, in Williamsburg, Virginia. 1982

Rachel Smith, oldest member of the third generation, now an entrepreneur in her own right. 1984

Richie Milligan, youngest member of the third generation, who loves swimming, golf, and soccer. 1989

Kim Harbert and Laura Smith, third generation, acting as greeters in our first shop. 1984

Jack Lawler, the first member of the fourth generation and our newest quilt tester. See other photos of him on pages 23 and 25. 2002

We think the Rubber Ducky Quilt makes a great theme for a baby shower. It would be great fun, and we have planned it for you, from the invitation to the menu.

Make the Rubber Ducky Quilt for the new baby. If the baby is going to be a girl, you might want to make the quilt in pinks and yellows. It would be very pretty.

Invitation

Here are several ways you can use the Rubber Ducky invitation on page 7. The invitation fits in a 4 x 5½″ envelope.

 Copy the invitation to yellow paper and write the shower information on the inside.

Copy it to white paper and use colored pencils or markers to decorate the duck.

Trace the duck outline onto fusible web. Fuse to a rectangle of yellow fabric slightly larger than the invitation. Fuse the fabric to a piece of lightweight tagboard. Cut out the shape of the duck invitation. Trace the wing, beak, eyes, and wheels on fusible web. Fuse to your choice of fabrics. Cut out and fuse in place. Fold in half at dotted line. Copy the inside information (bottom of this page) on the inside of the invitation.

Menu

- Goldfish Cracker Mix (page 7)
- Yellow sheet cake frosted with white icing and decorated with a rubber ducky
- Lemon sherbet
- Lemonade

Decorations

Purchase yellow rubber duckies for all guests. Print guests' names on the duckies with a permanent pen and use them for place cards.

For a centerpiece, fill a large glass bowl with water and float rubber duckies and clear ornaments with their stems removed (to look like bubbles).

Balloons in yellow, white, blue, and pink

Games

The Price is Right

Buy an assortment of small baby accessories such as nail clipper, nail scissors, pacifier, thermometer, diapers, t-shirts, baby bottles, tippy cup, spoon, jar of baby food, etc. Make a list of the items and prices. Shuffle the lists. Each guest tries to determine the correct price for each item. The one with the most correct answers wins a small prize, and all of the accessories go to the mother-to-be.

Guess the Goldfish

Fill a baby bottle with goldfish crackers and have guests guess the number. To make it even more fun, buy an extra large baby bottle at a party shop.

Guess the Size of the Mom-to-Be

This game only involves string and a pair of scissors. During the course of the shower, have each guest try to determine with string how big the mom-to-be is around the waist. Cut the string. After everyone has their string cut, use it to measure the mother's waist. The closest measurement wins a small prize.

Who Am I?

Place a famous baby or child's name on the back of each guest. Each guest tries to determine which baby they are by asking the other guests questions. This is a good ice breaker. To start you out, here is a list of good names. Shirley Temple; Campbell's Soup Kids; Morton Salt girl; Drew Barrymore; the Olson Twins; Elizabeth Taylor; JFK Junior; Caroline Kennedy; etc. It could also be television characters such as Builder Bob; Rainbow Brite; Strawberry Shortcake; My Little Pony; Lambchop; Mickey Mouse; Howdy Doody; Kookla, Fran, and Ollie; Teletubbies; etc.

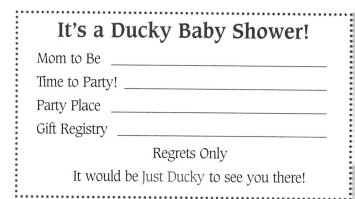

It's a Ducky Baby Shower!

Mom to Be _____

Time to Party! _____

Party Place _____

Gift Registry _____

Regrets Only

It would be Just Ducky to see you there!

Rubber Ducky Invitation

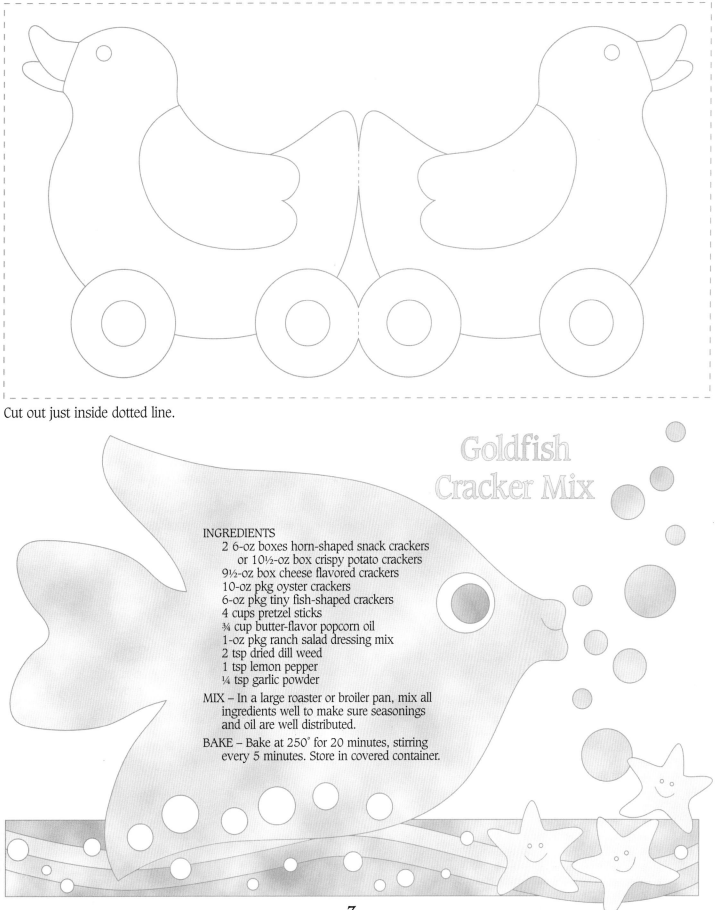

Cut out just inside dotted line.

Goldfish Cracker Mix

INGREDIENTS
  2 6-oz boxes horn-shaped snack crackers
      or 10½-oz box crispy potato crackers
  9½-oz box cheese flavored crackers
  10-oz pkg oyster crackers
  6-oz pkg tiny fish-shaped crackers
  4 cups pretzel sticks
  ¾ cup butter-flavor popcorn oil
  1-oz pkg ranch salad dressing mix
  2 tsp dried dill weed
  1 tsp lemon pepper
  ¼ tsp garlic powder

MIX – In a large roaster or broiler pan, mix all
  ingredients well to make sure seasonings
  and oil are well distributed.

BAKE – Bake at 250° for 20 minutes, stirring
  every 5 minutes. Store in covered container.

Other quilts in the book would make great themes for baby showers or birthday parties.

Just Ducky

Use this quilt instead of the Rubber Ducky quilt. All of the games and decorations could be the same, except use balloons in yellow, white, orange, and turquoise.

Space Dudes

This theme would be especially great for a youngster's birthday party. Use the invitation on page 9 and one of the characters from the quilt for the decoration on the cake. Buy lots of colorful balloons. Fill a container with brightly colored candy and play a variation of the Guess the Goldfish game (page 6).

ABCs and 123s or Snuggle Up Sampler

This theme would work great for a baby shower or an older child's birthday party.

Use the invitation on page 9. Hang pastel balloons. A fun game is to think up a baby name for each letter of the alphabet. Fill ice cream cones with cake batter to make cake cones or decorate a sheet cake to look like the quilt, using letters to spell out the baby's name.

Sleep Tight

This is a good quilt to make **at** the baby shower. The blocks are simple to make, and several people could work on it at the same time. Have a couple of cutters, some sewers, and some pressers. What a nice way to teach your friends how to do patchwork. Shower guests could also come with a finished block, then the blocks could be set together at the party.

CRANBERRY LEMONADE

COMBINE & STIR TO DISSOLVE SUGAR
1 quart cranberry juice, chilled
6-oz can frozen lemonade concentrate, undiluted
6-oz can frozen limeade concentrate, undiluted
¼ cup sugar (optional)

STIR IN 4 cups club soda, chilled

SERVE IN tall glasses with ice cubes

SERVES 10

Photocopy invitations to heavy paper and add detail with colored pencils or markers. Write your own party information on the reverse side. Invitations fit in 3⅞ x 7½" envelope.

ABCs and 123s
Invitation

9

Fabric Preparation

One hundred percent cotton fabrics are recommended for the quilts in this book. Determine if the fabrics are colorfast. Cut small scraps from each fabric and place these scraps into a clear glass of warm water one at a time. If the water stays clear, the fabric is colorfast. If there is a color change in the water, remove the excess dye by washing the fabric in warm water with a mild detergent. Rinse well. Retest and rewash as many times as necessary. If the fabrics are colorfast, washing is not required, but washing and tumble drying the fabric has the advantage of maximizing the shrinkage. Unwashed fabric retains its crispness and body, making it very easy to use, but the quilter must assume the risk of shrinkage and color bleeding. When using washed fabric, spray sizing or lightweight starch can be used to restore body.

NOTE: Several quilts in this book require usable fabric width to be 42½″. This means after washing and after removing selvages.

Rotary Cutting

A transparent rotary cutting ruler at least 12″ long, a rotary cutter with a sharp blade, and a self-healing cutting mat are needed. Unless otherwise indicated, cuts should be made from selvage to selvage. Reverse the directions if you are left handed.

1. Fold the fabric in half with the selvage edges even. Slide the selvages back and forth until there is no twist in the fabric, then lay it on the mat with the folded edge toward you. Fold the fabric in half again, matching the folded edge with the selvage edges. It is important that these folds are straight or the strips will be bowed. There are now four thicknesses of fabric.

2. Using a transparent rotary cutting ruler, match up a line on the ruler with the fold of the fabric. Make sure that the right edge of the ruler covers all four layers.

3. Trim off the excess fabric by holding the rotary cutting blade flat against the right edge of the ruler and place it just off the edge of fabric closest to you. To stabilize the ruler, place your hand so that two fingers extend off the left side of the ruler onto the

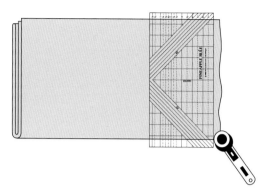

fabric. Push the rotary cutter away from you to cut off the right edge of fabric. The result is a straight edge from which to begin cutting strips.

4. Swing mat and fabric around 180°.

5. Position ruler so marking for desired strip width is even with just-cut edges of fabric. Keep top and bottom edges of fabric parallel to horizontal lines of ruler.

6. Cut away from you, then move strip carefully away from folded fabric to assist in placement of ruler for next cut.

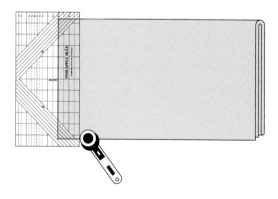

Cutting Tips

If many squares of the same size are needed, cut a strip the size of the square and then crosscut the strip into segments.

For half-square triangles, cut squares the size listed in the directions for each quilt and then line up the ruler from corner to corner and cut the squares into triangles.

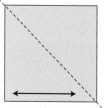

Straight Grain

For quarter-square triangles, cut squares the size listed in the directions for each quilt. Cut twice on the diagonal, not allowing the fabric to move between the first and second cuts.

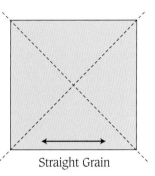
Straight Grain

Fusible Web Applique

1. Trace patterns the reverse of the direction wanted onto smooth, paper side of fusible web. For large shapes, cut out the center, leaving just a margin of web. **Note:** Patterns in this book have already been reversed for tracing.

2. Avoiding selvage, press fusible web to wrong side of fabric with rough side facing fabric. Cut out shapes.

3. Peel off paper. Position applique on background fabric and fuse in place. If design is layered, arrange all appliques before fusing. A great tool for building layered appliques before applying them to a background is an applique pressing sheet.

4. **Satin Stitch:** Place tear-away stabilizer under background fabric. Use a very short stitch length and a medium zigzag stitch width. Loosen top tension as needed to keep bobbin thread from showing on top of work. Keep threads of satin stitch at right angles to edge of applique by pivoting as needed. To make tapered points, reduce stitch width while sewing. To tie off threads, bring stitch width to zero, slide fabric to left or right, and take 6-8 stitches next to satin stitching. Tear away the stabilizer.

Invisible Open Zigzag: This is a fast way to secure edges of fused appliques without creating an outline of thread as in satin stitch. Use a narrow stitch width and a medium-short stitch length to create a small, open zigzag. Use nylon monofilament thread as the top thread only.

Machine Blanket Stitch: Some machines have a squared-off zigzag stitch called a blanket or buttonhole stitch (not the settings used for garment buttonholes, but a decorative stitch). Refer to individual sewing machine manuals for directions. No stabilizer is needed behind the background fabric. Many threads can be used for this stitch, each creating a different look. Jeans thread used with large machine blanket stitch settings looks just like hand buttonhole stitching. Experiment with other decorative machine stitches.

Piecing & Pressing

1. Establish a ¼″ seam allowance on your sewing machine. If the machine does not have a quarter-inch presser foot or adjustable needle positions, place a rotary cutting ruler under the sewing machine needle. Line up the ruler with the first ¼″ line directly under the needle. Lower the needle carefully. Make sure the ruler is square to the front of the machine. Place a piece of masking tape along the edge of the ruler on the throat plate and use it as a guide for the edge of your fabric.

2. Use a light neutral cotton thread when piecing most fabrics. If all fabrics are dark, use a dark thread. Thread in the top and bobbin should be the same type to make the most consistent stitches.

3. Place the pieces to be joined right sides together. Pin, matching seam lines, and sew, using an accurate ¼″ seam allowance, and a straight stitch, 10-12 stitches per inch. A short stitch length will make it unnecessary to backstitch at the beginning and ending of seams. Press seam allowances to one side, usually toward the darker fabric unless otherwise noted. If you have trouble with the loose threads at the beginning of a seam or with the points of a triangle being pushed down into the throat plate, start sewing on a folded fabric scrap and then feed the pieces under the presser foot.

4. Use an iron set for cotton and an up-and-down motion rather than a pushing motion. The goal is to set the seams and remove wrinkles without distortion. With the dark fabric on top, press the pieces flat, as they were sewn, to set the stitches. Then, without moving the fabric, fold the top fabric over the stitching line and press the seam. This works well for long strips as well as small pieces.

Piecing Tips

Chain piecing saves time and thread. After sewing a seam, immediately feed in a new set of pieces without lifting the presser foot or clipping threads. Sew as many sets as possible in this manner, and then clip them apart. On long strips, take care not to pull or stretch the strips or they may become wavy.

Where two seams meet, position one seam allowance in one direction and one seam allowance in the opposite direction. Push the seams together tightly; they will hold each other in place, making it unnecessary to pin.

When crossing the seam intersections of triangles, aim for the point where the seam lines intersect. This will avoid cutting off the points in the patchwork design.

If one edge appears to be larger, put that side next to the feed-dog of the machine so the excess will be eased into the seam without leaving tucks.

Making strip sets is an efficient and accurate way to prepare parts for nine-patches and some other patchwork units. The method involves cutting strips, stitching them together, crosscutting them into segments, and using the segments to assemble units or blocks.

Set A   Set B

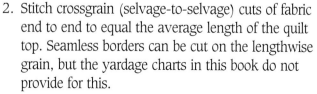

Stairstep Borders

1. To determine the length of the side borders, measure the length of the quilt from cut edge to cut edge in at least three places. Do not measure along the edges of the quilt as the edges can be stretched and the measurement may be longer than one taken across the center. Average these measurements.

Measure

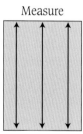

2. Stitch crossgrain (selvage-to-selvage) cuts of fabric end to end to equal the average length of the quilt top. Seamless borders can be cut on the lengthwise grain, but the yardage charts in this book do not provide for this.

3. Fold one side border and one side of quilt top into quarters and mark with pins. Matching marked points, pin border to quilt, right sides together. This distributes any ease along the entire edge of the quilt.

Mark & Stitch

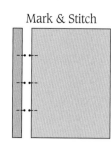

4. Stitch border to quilt. If one edge (quilt top or border) is slightly longer, put that side against the feed-dog, and the excess will be eased into the seam. Repeat for other side of quilt.

5. Repeat measuring and stitching process for top and bottom borders of quilt.

Repeat For Top & Bottom

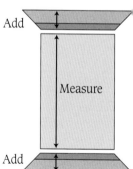

6. For a second border, simply measure down the center of the first border. Stitch the side borders to the quilt, then measure for top and bottom borders.

7. If a third border is needed, measure and stitch the same way.

8. Press border seams toward outside edge of quilt.

Mitered Borders

1. Measure and prepare borders

   a. To determine the length to prepare the side borders, measure the quilt length without borders as described in Step 1 of Stairstep Borders above. Add to this measurement, double the width of all planned borders of the quilt, then add 2-4″ extra (yardage charts include this extra fabric).

Add
Measure
Add

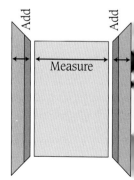

   b. To determine the length to prepare the top and bottom borders, measure the quilt top width without borders and add double the width of all planned borders of the quilt plus 2-4″ extra.

Add   Measure   Add

c. Stitch crossgrain cuts of fabric together, if necessary, to make the needed lengths, or cut seamless border strips on the lengthwise grain. If the quilt has more than one border, sew individual borders for each side together first to make complete border units. Press seam allowances toward outside edge of quilt.

2. Pin and Stitch Borders to Quilt

a. Measure the length of the quilt without borders from seam line to seam line by measuring the center of the quilt in several places. Do not measure along the edge of the quilt as it is often stretched and the measurement will be longer than a measurement taken across the center. Average these measurements.

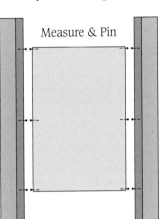
Measure & Pin

b. Find the center of the long inside edge of one side border unit and mark it with a pin. Measure from the pin each direction one-half the quilt length measurement minus ¼″ and mark with pins. These marks correspond to the corner seam intersections on the quilt.

c. Find center of quilt side by folding and mark it with a pin. Pin side border unit to quilt side, right sides together, matching corner seam intersections on quilt to corresponding marked points on border; match centers. Pin at intervals.

d. Stitch, beginning and ending stitching at corner seam intersections.

e. Repeat for other side, then for top and bottom.

3. Lay a corner of the quilt, right side up, on ironing board. The quilt may be pinned to the ironing board to keep it from falling off or being distorted. With borders overlapping, fold one border under at a 45° angle. Match the seams and work with it until it matches perfectly. The outer edges should be very

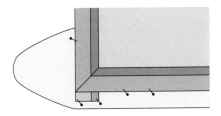

square and without any extra fullness. Border seams should create a 90° angle. Press this fold.

4. Flip outside edge of border with pressed fold over to other outside edge of border, right sides together; pin along pressed fold, placing pins parallel to the fold line. Open and check for accuracy before stitching. Stitch from inner corner to outside of quilt, backstitching at both ends of seam. It may be helpful to baste this seam first.

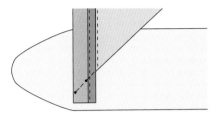

5. Lay mitered corner of quilt on ironing board right side up to see if seams match, Press. Trim seam to ¼″. Repeat for other three corners.

Machine Quilting

A quilt is much easier to mark before it is layered. There are a number of good quality marking pens and pencils available. Experiment with several to find one that is easy to use and is removable. Select a quilting design and mark the top lightly.

For quilts that require pieced backings, piece the backing either horizontally or vertically (charts include this information for each quilt). Allow at least 2″ to extend beyond the quilt top. Basting joins the three layers together in preparation for quilting. All of the quilts in this book have been machine quilted.

Safety pinning or spray basting works well for machine quilting. For safety pin basting, use one-inch safety pins placed four to six inches apart in spots where they will not be in the way of planned quilting lines. If spray basting, lightly spray the wrong side of the backing fabric and anchor it flat to the floor—either by taping to a hard floor or pinning into the carpet. Place the batting on the backing and smooth it out. Then lightly spray the wrong side of the quilt top, center it on the batting, and smooth it out. Release backing from floor and work out any wrinkles on the back.

For straight-line machine quilting, use an even-feed or walking foot. For free-motion quilting, use a darning or quilting foot and lower or cover the feed-dog. If you haven't machine quilted before, it is wise to stitch a practice piece first. Machine quilting takes practice, and a class at a local quilt store is a good investment.

Binding

FOLDED MITER

1. Trim batting and backing even with quilt top.

2. Cut 2½″ strips on the crossgrain of the fabric. Stitch end to end to fit all the way around the quilt.

3. Press binding in half lengthwise, wrong sides together. Leaving a 6″ tail of binding and using a ⅜″ seam allowance, begin stitching binding to right side of quilt at least 12″ from one of the corners. Stop stitching at seam intersection of first corner. Leave needle in fabric and pivot quilt 90°. Backstitch to edge.

Pivot & then backstitch at seam intersection

Right Side

4. Pull quilt slightly away from machine, leaving threads attached. Make a 45° fold in binding.

Make 45° fold

5. Fold again, aligning second fold with top edge of quilt and raw edges of binding even with right raw edge of quilt.

Fold again

6. Resume stitching at top edge using a ⅜″ seam allowance.

Resume stitching

7. After making all four mitered corners, stop stitching 6″ from where you started. Take quilt out of machine. Lay ends of binding along unstitched edge of quilt. Trim ends so they overlap by ½″.

8. Unfold binding and pull ends away from quilt. Place ends of binding right sides together; stitch with ¼″ seam; finger press seam open. Refold binding and place it along unstitched edge of quilt. Stitch remaining section of binding to quilt.

9. Turn binding to back and hand stitch folded edge to cover stitched line. To evenly distribute bulk, fold each corner miter in the opposite direction from which it was folded and stitched on the front.

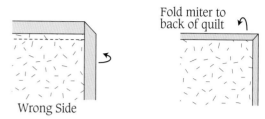

Fold miter to back of quilt

Wrong Side

STITCHED MITER

1. Prepare binding for each side of quilt, pressed in half lengthwise, wrong sides together, allowing 2-3″ extra length.

2. Stitch binding to each side of quilt separately, using a ⅜″ seam allowance. Start and stop stitching at seam intersection of corner.

Backstitch at seam intersection

Right Side

3. Fold binding out, overlapping the two strips at right angles. Draw a line from seam intersection on quilt out to edges of binding strips as shown. Draw a line at right angles to first line, as shown.

Mark

Wrong Side

4. Fold corner of quilt, wrong sides together, placing binding strips right sides together. Stitch as shown.

Stitch

Right Side

5. Trim seam allowance to ¼″. Trim point.

6. Turn to back of quilt, pushing out corner, and hand stitch folded edge of binding to cover stitched line.

Nothing says "I love you" like a quilt. The charts for many of the quilts include yardage requirements for CRIB size, CUDDLE size (lap or throw), and TWIN size. Read charts and directions thoroughly before proceeding. Directions include a scale drawing of the quilt in the size made for the photo. Refer to *Quilting Techniques*, page 6, for help with specific quiltmaking methods.

Because of fabric shrinkage, cutting techniques, and individual cutting discrepancies, the yardage for these quilts has been adjusted slightly upward. It is always a good idea to cut the entire quilt as soon as possible so that more fabric can be purchased if necessary. Where appropriate, border and binding fabric have been listed separately from fabric specified for patchwork to allow for individual choices. Sashing, borders, and binding are made with crossgrain, selvage-to-selvage, strips. Use the border directions in *Quilting Techniques* for measuring and stitching borders that perfectly fit the quilt you have made.

Backings have **H or V** following the yardage to indicate whether to piece them **horizontally or vertically**.

Finishing Steps for All Quilts

See Quilting Techniques for more detailed descriptions.

1. Press quilt top well.
2. Mark quilt for quilting, if desired.
3. Piece backing if necessary.
4. Layer backing, batting, and quilt top. Baste.
5. Quilt by hand or machine, or tie.
6. Bind.

Just Ducky

BLOCK SIZE: 10″. Photo is of the CRIB size quilt. Applique patterns are on insert.
Use 42-44″-wide fabric. When strips appear in the cutting list, cut crossgrain strips (selvage to selvage).

		CRIB	CUDDLE	TWIN
Quilt Size		50x60″	62x72″	70x92″
Blocks Set		3x4	4x5	5x7
Total # of Blocks		12	20	35

Yardage

	CRIB	CUDDLE	TWIN
White - patchwork	2¾ yd	4 yd	5⅝ yd
Yellows - patchwork & applique	⅜ yd each of 6	½ yd each of 6	⅝ yd each of 6
Dark yellow - mama duck	¼ yd	¼ yd	¼ yd
Light yellow - baby ducks	⅙ yd	⅙ yd	⅙ yd
Orange - beaks & wheels	⅛ yd	⅛ yd	⅛ yd
Blue - hearts, duck platform, rope, eyes	⅛ yd	⅛ yd	⅛ yd
Binding	⅝ yd	⅝ yd	¾ yd
Backing	3¼ yd H	4 yd H	5⅞ yd V
Batting	54x64″	68x78″	76x98″

Cutting

*Cut these squares in HALF diagonally.

			CRIB	CUDDLE	TWIN
White					
	Blocks, Border 2	2½ x4½″	48	80	140
		*2⅞″ squares	*124	*184	*288
	Border 1	2½″ strips	4	-	4 - sides
		3½″ strips	-	5	3 - top & bottom
	Border 2	2½″ squares	2	2	2
	Border 3	6½″ strips	4	6	7
		6½″ squares	4	4	4
Yellow					
	Blocks	2½″ squares	12	20	35
	Blocks	*4⅞″ squares	*24	*40	*70
	Blocks, Border 2	*2⅞″ squares	*76	*104	*148
	Appliques	Use photo, diagrams, and pattern pieces as guides			
Binding		2½″ strips	6	7	9

Continued on page 53.

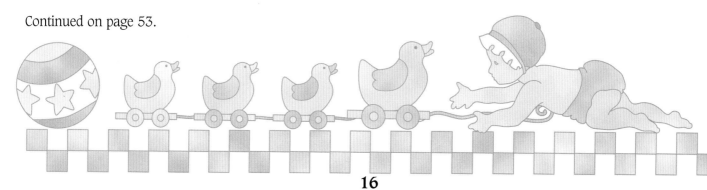

Just Ducky - Facing Page

QUILT SIZE: 45x53″
BLOCK SIZE: 7½″
30 blocks set 5x6
Use 42-44″-wide fabric. When strips appear in the cutting list, cut crossgrain strips (selvage to selvage). Applique patterns are on insert.

Yardage

Pastel prints	¼ yd each of 15
Pastel monotones	¼ yd each of 15
Border 1	⅓ yd
Border 2	⅝ yd
Binding	⅝ yd
Backing	3 yd H
Batting	49x57″

Cutting

Pastel prints
  Cut in order from each fabric:

5½″ square	1
applique	1
3x5½″	1
3x8″	2
3x10½″	1

Pastel monotones
  Cut in order from each fabric:

5½″ square	1
applique	1
3x5½″	1
3x8″	2
3x10½″	1

Border 1	1½″ strips	5
Border 2	3½″ strips	5
Binding	2½″ strips	6

Directions

Use ¼″ seam allowance. Diagrams on page 62.

1. BLOCKS

  a. Choose 3 fabrics for each block—one 5½″ square for center and 2 pairs of rectangles, 1 pair for sides (3x8″ and 3x10½″) and 1 pair for top and bottom (3x8″ and 3x5½″).

  b. Stitch 3x5½″ piece to top of 5½″ square. Press. Stitch 3x8″ piece to right side of square. Press. Stitch 3x8″ piece to bottom of square. Press. Stitch 3x10½″ piece to left side of square. Press.

  c. Applique blocks with alphabet, star, and numbers. See *Quilting Techniques*, page 11, for fusible web applique directions.

  d. Make 8″ plastic template. Matching center of block and center of template, cut tilted blocks as shown in diagram on page 62.

2. ASSEMBLY: Place blocks in alphabetical order with star and number blocks at end—6 rows of 5 blocks each. Stitch blocks into rows. Stitch rows together. Press.

3. BORDER: See *Stairstep Borders*, page 12.

4. Refer to *Finishing Steps for All Quilts*, page 15. Quilt in photo is machine quilted in the ditch and close to appliques. Border 1 is quilted with a wavy line, and Border 2 is quilted with a scroll pattern.

Continued on page 62.

ABCs & 123s - Facing Page

BLOCK SIZE: 6″. Photo is of the TWIN size quilt.
Use 42-44″-wide fabric. When strips appear in the cutting list, cut crossgrain strips (selvage to selvage).

	CRIB	CUDDLE	TWIN
Quilt Size	44x56″	56x68″	66x90″
Blocks Set	6x8	8x10	9x13
Total # of Blocks	48	80	117

Yardage

	CRIB	CUDDLE	TWIN
White	1⅝ yd	2¼ yd	3½ yd
Pastel prints	⅙ yd each of 10 or more	⅙ yd each of 16 or more	⅙ yd each of 24 or more
Green mottled solid	¾ yd	⅞ yd	1⅛ yd
Backing	3 yd H	3¾ yd H	5¾ yd V
Batting	48x60″	62x74″	72x96″

Cutting

*Cut these squares in HALF diagonally.

White		CRIB	CUDDLE	TWIN
Blocks	4¾″ squares	48	80	117
Border 2	3½″ strips	5	6	-
	5½″ strips	-	-	8

Pastel prints				
Blocks	*3⅞ ″ squares	*96	*160	*234

Green mottled				
Border 1	1½″ strips	5	6	7
Binding	2½″ strips	6	7	9

Continued on page 54.

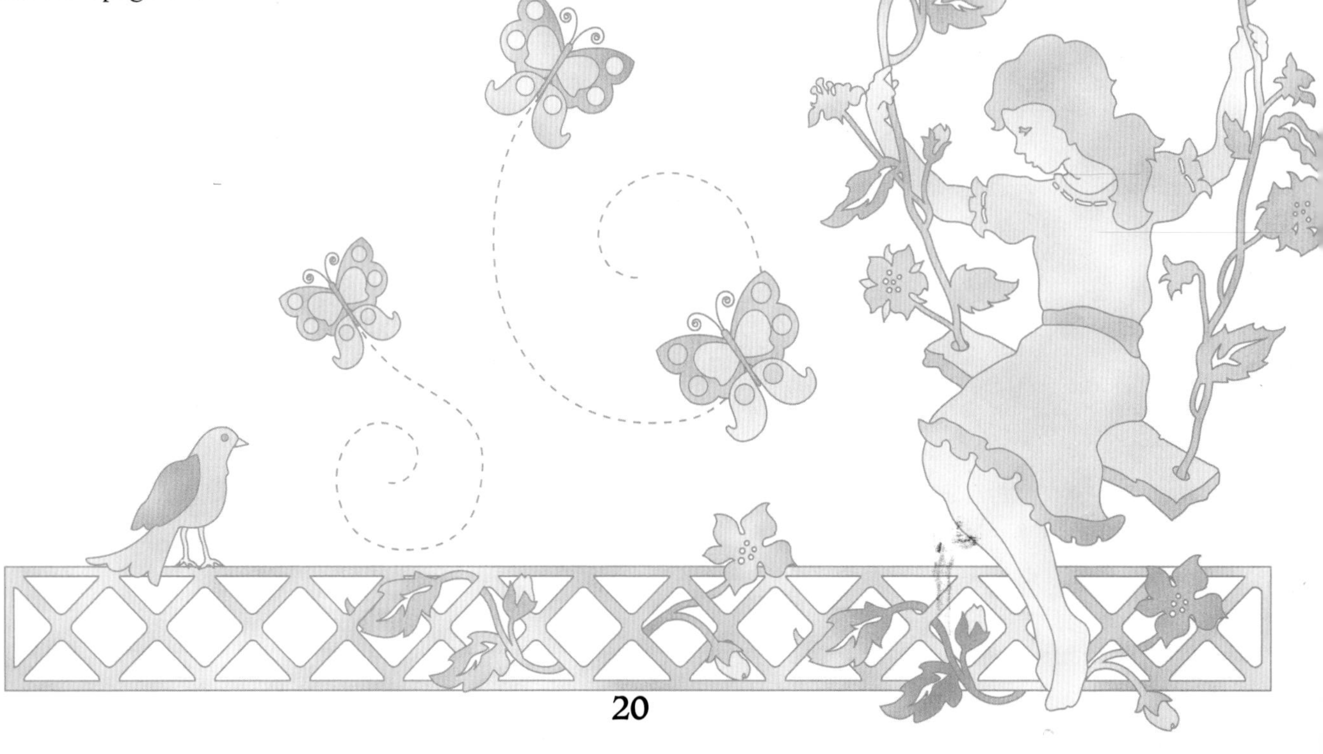

Pretty Posies - Facing Page
Shhh...Baby Sleeping - Page 48

QUILT SIZE: 55x68″
BLOCK SIZES: 9″, 4½″, & others
Use 42-44″-wide fabric. When strips appear in the cutting list, cut crossgrain strips (selvage to selvage). Applique patterns are on insert.

Yardage

Pastel monotones	⅝ yd each of 10
Rainbow print	⅓ yd
Border 1	½ yd
Border 2	⅞ yd
Binding	⅝ yd
Backing	3¾ yd H
Batting	61x74″

Cutting

See diagram on page 64.

NOTE: Use fabrics as desired. Some pieces listed are parts of larger units and need to be color coordinated with other pieces.

*Cut these squares in HALF diagonally.

Pastel monotones & rainbow print

Piece/Unit 1	2″ squares	12 each of 2 colors
Piece/Unit 2	2″ squares	20 - color 1
		16 - color 2
Piece/Unit 3	5″ squares	8 for 4-patches - color 1
		8 for 4-patches - color 2
		4 for single-square units
Piece/Unit 4	*5⅜″ squares	*2 each of 6 colors
Piece/Unit 5	5x9½″	5
Piece/Unit 6	9½x18½″	3
Piece/Unit 7	9½″ squares	11
Piece/Unit 8	8x18½″	2

Appliques	large heart	3
	small heart	8
	lge. pointy star	4
	star centers	4
	lge. fat star	6
	sm. fat star	1
	ABC, 123	1 set each
Border 1	2″ strips	6
Border 2	4″ strips	6
Binding	2½″ strips	7

Directions

Use ¼″ seam allowance. Diagrams on page 64.

1. PATCHWORK: Make units shown in diagrams. Press.

2. APPLIQUE: Applique units as shown in diagram. See *Quilting Techniques*, page 11, for fusible web applique directions.

3. ASSEMBLY: Stitch units into panels as shown in diagram. Stitch panels together. Press.

4. BORDERS: See *Stairstep Borders*, page 12.

5. Refer to *Finishing Steps for All Quilts*, page 15. Quilt in photo is outline and ditch quilted by machine. Double-line hearts and stars are quilted in the large plain blocks. Border 1 is quilted with a wavy line, and Border 2 is quilted with a heart pattern.

Continued on page 64.

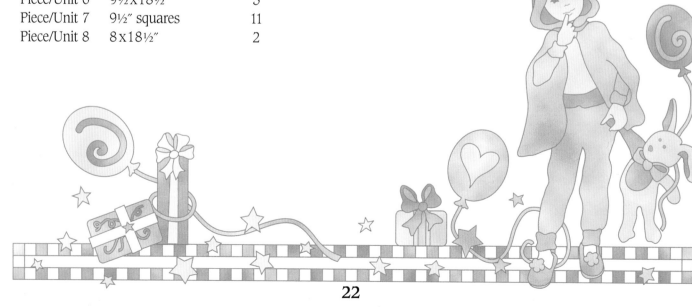

Snuggle Up - Facing Page

Double Dipping - Page 49   Pentagon Ball - Page 70

Fish Frenzy

BLOCK SIZE: 12″. Photo is of the CUDDLE size quilt. Applique patterns are on insert.
Use 42-44″-wide fabric. When strips appear in the cutting list, cut crossgrain strips (selvage to selvage).
NOTE: If using a half-square triangle method of your own choice, more yardage may be required.

	CRIB	CUDDLE	TWIN
Quilt Size	40x57″	57x74″	74x91″
Total # of Appliqued Blocks	7	17	31

Yardage

	CRIB	CUDDLE	TWIN
Black - setting triangles, small triangles	1½ yd	2½ yd	3½ yd
Light monotones green, purple, blue, pink, turquoise			
Small triangles, appliques	⅓ yd each of 4 or more	⅓ yd each of 6 or more	⅓ yd each of 9 or more
Yellow - starfish & fish parts	¼ yd	½ yd	¾ yd
Medium monotones green, purple, blue, pink, turquoise			
Small triangles, block backgrounds	⅓ yd each of 4 or more	⅓ yd each of 9 or more	⅓ yd each of 16 or more
Border 1 - turquoise	½ yd	⅝ yd	¾ yd
Border 2 - purple	⅜ yd	½ yd	⅝ yd
Binding	⅝ yd	⅝ yd	¾ yd
Backing	2¾ yd H	3¾ yd H	5¾ yd V
Batting	44x61″	63x80″	80x97″

Cutting

*Cut these squares in HALF diagonally. **Cut these squares in QUARTERS diagonally.

		CRIB	CUDDLE	TWIN
Black				
Setting triangles	**12½″	**3	**4	**5
Small triangles	*2⅞″ squares	*125	*247	*409
Light monotones				
Small triangles	*2⅞″ squares	*63	*124	*205
Applique		4 fish	9 fish	16 fish
Yellow		3 starfish & fish parts	8 starfish & fish parts	15 starfish & fish parts
Medium monotones				
Block bkgrnd. cut first	8½″ squares	7	17	31
Small triangles	*2⅞″ squares	*63	*124	*205
Border 1	2½″ strips	5	7	8
Border 2	1¾″ strips	5	7	9
Binding	2½″ strips	6	7	9

Continued on page 57.

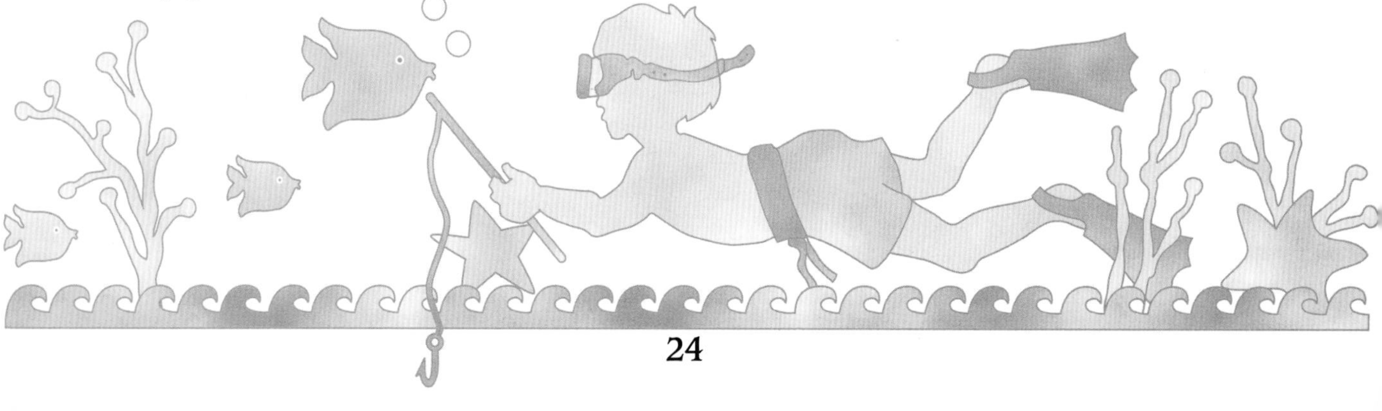

Fish Frenzy - Facing Page

Beanbag Game Board - Page 74   Fish Frenzy Beanbags - Page 74

Forever Stripes

QUILT SIZE: 65x90"
PILLOW TOPPER SIZE: 65x38"
Use 42-44"-wide fabric. When strips appear in the cutting list, cut crossgrain strips (selvage to selvage). Applique pattern is on insert.

Yardage

PILLOW TOPPER
Blue	2 yd
White	¼ yd
Binding	⅝ yd
Backing	2 yd
Batting	42x69"

QUILT
Red prints	¼ yd each of 22
White-on-whites	⅜ yd each of 9
Backing	5¾ yd V
Batting	71x96"

Cutting

PILLOW TOPPER
Blue	40x65"	1
White	hearts	5
Binding	2½" strips	6

QUILT
Red prints	5½" strips	1 from each fabric
White-on-whites	5½" strips	2 from each fabric

Directions

Use ¼" seam allowance. Diagrams on page 63.

1. PILLOW TOPPER

   a. Applique hearts to blue panel: Place one in center of panel; place two to each side of center heart spaced 5½" apart. See *Quilting Techniques*, page 11 for fusible web applique directions.

2. QUILT

   a. Cut red strips into segments of varying lengths from approximately 6" to approximately 12".

   b. Stitch segments together into 7 vertical rows 90" long, trimming length when needed and varying placement of fabrics and sizes of pieces. Press.

   c. Repeat Steps a. and b. to make 6 white rows.

   d. Stitch red and white rows together, referring to photo and diagram. Press.

3. Refer to *Finishing Steps for All Quilts*, page 15. Pillow topper in photo is machine quilted with loops and hearts. The quilt is quilted with loops and stars.

   Binding: For quilt, cut leftover red rectangles lengthwise into two 2½" pieces each. Stitch enough pieces end to end to make approximately 320" long. Press seam allowances open. Continue with binding directions in *Quilting Techniques*, page 14, for both topper and quilt.

Continued on page 63.

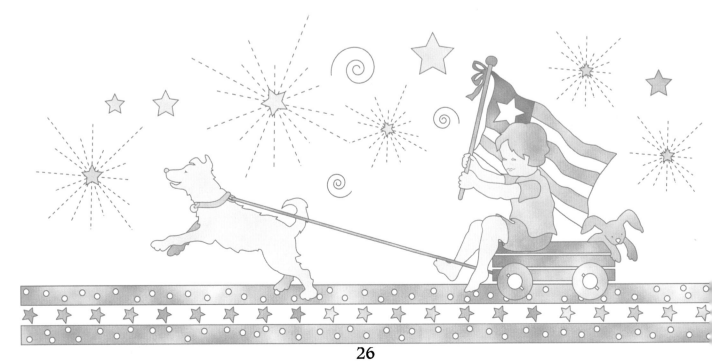

26

Forever Stripes - Facing Page
Field of Stars - Page 50

Sweet Hearts

QUILT SIZE: 60x75″

Use 42-44″-wide fabric. When strips appear in the cutting list, cut crossgrain strips (selvage to selvage). Applique pattern is on insert.

Yardage

White - 42½″ usable width needed	4⅜ yd
Dark pink	1⅜ yd
Backing	4 yd H
Batting	66x81″

Cutting

*Cut these squares in HALF diagonally.

White

Center panel	42½ x 57½″	1
Borders 1 & 3	2″ squares	8
Borders 1 & 3	*2⅜″ squares	*140
Border 2	2″ strips	6
Border 4	5″ strips	7
Binding	2½″ strips	7

Dark pink

Borders 1 & 3	*2⅜″ squares	*140
	hearts	50

Directions

Use ¼″ seam allowance. Diagrams on page 62.

1. CENTER PANEL

   a. Lightly mark right side of panel with horizontal and vertical lines using diagram on page 62.

   b. Applique hearts to panel, centered on intersections of lines as shown in diagram. See *Quilting Techniques*, page 11, for fusible web applique directions.

2. BORDERS 1 & 3: Make 280 half-square triangle units.

3. BORDER 1

   a. Stitch 38 half-square triangle units together to make side border, changing direction at center. Make 2. Stitch to quilt. Press.

   b. Stitch 28 units together to make top/bottom border, changing direction at center. Stitch white squares to each end. Make 2. Stitch to quilt. Press.

4. BORDER 2: See *Stairstep Borders*, page 12.

5. BORDER 3: Repeat Step 3a. using 42 units. Repeat Step 3b. using 32 units.

6. BORDER 4: See *Stairstep Borders*, page 12.

7. Refer to *Finishing Steps for All Quilts*, page 15. Quilt in photo is machine quilted with heart/feather designs on the center panel and a feather vine in Border 4. Sawtooth borders are ditch quilted, and a wavy line is quilted along the center of Border 2.

Continued on page 62.

Sweet Hearts - Facing Page

Fuzzy Wuzzy

QUILT SIZE: 49x 66″

Use 42-44″-wide fabric. When strips appear in the cutting list, cut crossgrain strips (selvage to selvage). NOTE: Use flannel and don't wash it before making the quilt. When the quilt is finished, wash it and dry it in a dryer to fringe the raw edges.

Yardage

Yellow - large squares	1¼ yd
Plaid - large squares, Border	1⅜ yd
Purple - small squares, strip sets, Border corners	⅝ yd
Pink - small squares, strip sets	¾ yd
Teal #1 - strip sets	¼ yd
Teal #2 - center panel background 42½″ usable width needed	1⅞ yd
Blue - strip sets	⅜ yd
Light blue - strip sets	¼ yd
Binding	⅝ yd
Backing	3⅜ yd H
Batting	55x72″

Cutting

Yellow	4½″ squares	58
Plaid	4½″ squares	18
	4″ strips - border	6
Purple	2″ squares	76
	1½″ strips	3
	4″ squares - border	4
Pink	2″ squares	76
	1½″ strips	9
Teal #1	1½″ strips	3
Teal #2	42½x 59½″	1
Blue	1½″ strips	6
Light blue	1½″ strips	3
Binding	2½″ strips	6-7

Directions

Use ¼″ seam allowance. Diagrams on page 65.

1. SQUARE UNITS
   a. Stack in order: large plaid square, small purple square, and small pink square, centered, all right side up. Topstitch with a narrow open zigzag ¼″ from edges of small squares.
   b. Repeat with large yellow, small pink and small purple squares.
2. STRIP SETS & RAIL FENCE UNITS
   a. Make 3 Strip Set A with pink–teal #1–blue–pink strips. Press.
   b. Make 3 Strip Set B with purple–light blue–pink–blue. Press.
   c. Crosscut strip sets into 4½″ segments.
   d. Stitch 1 Segment A and 1 Segment B together as shown. Make 24.
3. CENTER PANEL ASSEMBLY
   a. Stitch yellow square units into sets of 3 and 4 as shown.
   b. Stitch units together in diagonal rows as shown. Press. NOTE: Diagrams show symmetrical placement of Rail Fence units, but they can be placed asymmetrically (randomly) as shown in the photo.
4. CENTER PANEL BACKGROUND
   a. Lay center panel background on floor, right side up. Lay center panel on background, right side up, centered. Pin well.
   b. Topstitch edge of center panel to background with a narrow open zigzag ¼″ from edge.
   c. If desired, from wrong side, trim background away from center of quilt top.

Continued on page 65.

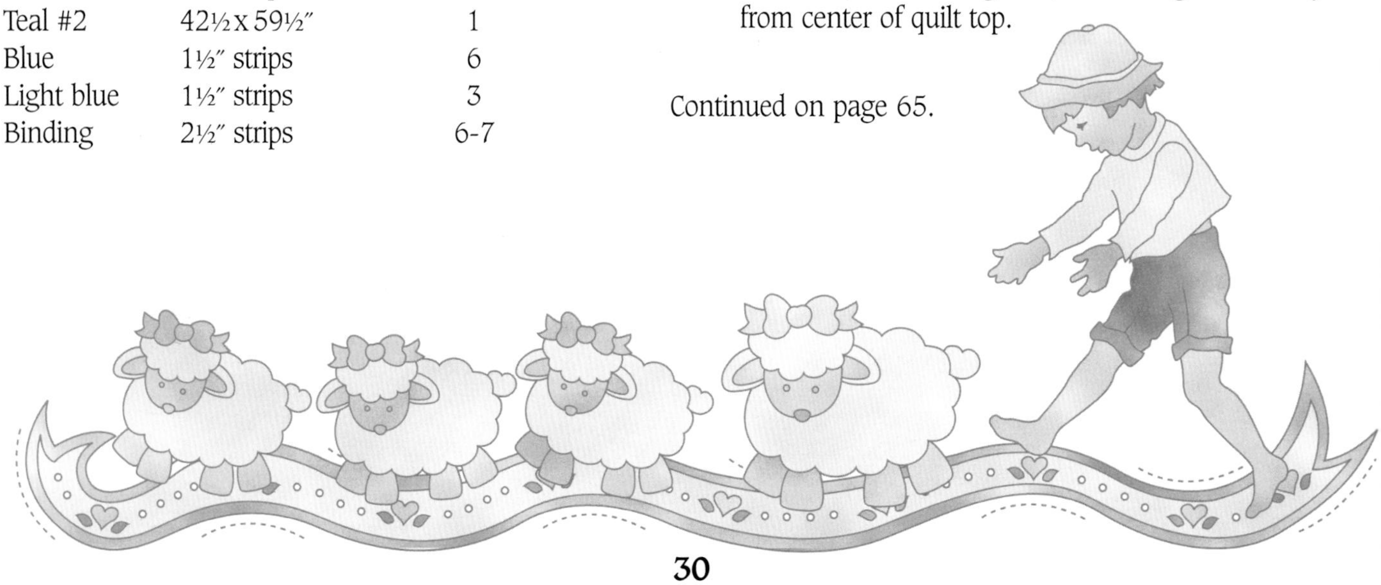

Fuzzy Wuzzy - Facing Page

Baby Steps

BLOCK SIZE: 6″. Photo is of the CRIB size quilt.

Use 42-44″-wide fabric. When strips appear in the cutting list, cut crossgrain strips (selvage to selvage).

	CRIB	CUDDLE	TWIN
Quilt Size	46x58″	52x73″	69x96″
Total # of Units	18 A	27 A	48 A
	30 B	54 B	96 B
	17 C	27 C	48 C

Yardage

	CRIB	CUDDLE	TWIN
Fuchsia - 42½″ usable width needed	1 yd	1⅜ yd	2 yd
Green - 42½″ usable width needed	¾ yd	1⅛ yd	1⅞ yd
Blue - 42½″ usable width needed	1⅛ yd	1½ yd	2⅛ yd
Purple - 42½″ usable width needed	⅔ yd	⅞ yd	1½ yd
Yellow - 42½″ usable width needed	½ yd	⅝ yd	1 yd
Backing	3⅛ yd H	3½ yd H	6⅛ yd V
Batting	50x62″	58x79″	75x102″

Cutting

		CRIB	CUDDLE	TWIN
Fuchsia				
Unit C	2½″ strips	1	2	3
Border	5½″ strips	5	6	-
	6½″ strips	-	-	8
Green				
Unit A	3½″ strips	3	5	8
Unit C	2½″ strips	2	4	6
Row 2	3½″ squares	16	22	42
Blue				
Unit A	3½″ strips	3	5	8
Unit C	2½″ strips	2	4	6
Binding	2½″ strips	6	7	9
Purple				
Unit B	3½″ strips	2	2	4
Unit C	2½″ strips	2	4	6
Row 2	3½″ squares	16	20	42
Yellow				
Unit B	3½″ strips	2	2	4
Unit C	2½″ strips	2	4	6

Continued on page 55.

Baby Steps - Facing Page

BLOCK SIZE: 9″. Photo is of the CRIB size quilt.
Use 42-44″-wide fabric. When strips appear in the cutting list, cut crossgrain strips (selvage to selvage).

	CRIB	CUDDLE	TWIN
Quilt Size	48 x 58″	58 x 68″	72 x 90″
Blocks Set	4 x 5	5 x 6	6 x 8
Total # of Pinwheel Blocks	10	15	24
Total # of Four-Patch Blocks	10	15	24

Yardage

	CRIB	CUDDLE	TWIN
Blue/yellow print - Pinwheel block	⅝ yd	⅞ yd	1⅜ yd
Blue monotone - Nine-Patch unit, Border 2	⅔ yd	1 yd	1⅜ yd
Green monotone - Nine-Patch unit	½ yd	¾ yd	1 yd
Yellow monotone - block bkg. & borders	2⅜ yd	3 yd	4⅜ yd
Binding	⅝ yd	⅝ yd	¾ yd
Backing	3¼ yd H	3⅞ yd H	5¾ yd V
Batting	52 x 62″	64 x 74″	78 x 96″

Cutting

*Cut these squares in HALF diagonally.

Blue/yellow print		CRIB	CUDDLE	TWIN
Pinwheel blocks	*5⅜″ squares	*20	*30	*48
Blue monotone				
Nine-Patch units	2″ strips	4	7	11
Border 2	*2⅞″ squares	*43	*53	*69
Green monotone	2″ strips	5	8	13
	2½″ squares	4	4	4
Yellow monotone				
Pinwheel blocks	*5⅜″ squares	*20	*30	*48
Four-Patch blocks	5″ squares	20	30	48
Border 1	1½″ strips	3	-	-
	2″ strips	2	3	-
	2½″ strips	-	3	-
	3½″ strips	-	-	7
Border 2	*2⅞″ squares	*43	*53	*69
Border 3	3½″ strips	5-6	7	-
	4½″ strips	-	-	8
Binding	2½″ strips	6	7	9

Continued on page 59.

Sweet Dreams - Facing Page

osted Flowers

BLOCK SIZE: 12″. Photo is of the CRIB size quilt. Applique patterns are on insert.

Use 42-44″-wide fabric. When strips appear in the cutting list, cut crossgrain strips (selvage to selvage).

NOTE: If using a half-square triangle method of your own choice, more yardage may be required.

	CRIB	CUDDLE	TWIN
Quilt Size	48x48″	48x65″	71x88″
Blocks Set on Point	2x2	2x3	3x4
Total # of Blocks	5	8	18

Yardage

	CRIB	CUDDLE	TWIN
White	1¾ yd	1⅞ yd	3 yd
Pink - 2 fabrics for block backgrounds	⅓ yd each	⅓ yd each	⅞ yd & ⅝ yd
Pastel prints			
Mostly pinks, some yellow, blue, green	⅛ yd each of 12 or more	⅛ yd each of 18 or more	¼ yd each of 18 or more
Applique - 3-4 pinks, 1 green	⅙ yd each	¼ yd each 1 green, 1 pink	½ yd each 1 green, 1 pink
		⅙ yd ea. 2 pinks	⅙ yd 2-3 pinks
Borders 1 & 2	⅓ yd each of 2	⅜ yd each of 2	⅝ yd each of 2
Binding	⅝ yd	⅝ yd	¾ yd
Backing	3⅛ yd V	3¼ yd H	5⅝ yd V
Batting	52x52″	54x71″	77x94″

Cutting

*Cut these squares in HALF diagonally.   **Cut these squares in QUARTERS diagonally.

White		CRIB	CUDDLE	TWIN
Triangle units	*2⅞″ squares	*20	*25	*35
Setting triangles	**12½″ squares	**1	**2	**3
Setting triangles	*6½″ squares	*2	*2	*2
Border 3	5½″ strips	6	7	-
	7½″	-	-	9
Pink - blocks	8½″ squares	4+1	4 of each fabric	10+8
Pastel prints				
Triangle units	*2⅞″ squares	*148	*225	*459
Borders 1 & 2	1½″ strips	5 of each fabric	6 of each fabric	-
	2″ strips	-	-	8 of each fabric
Applique		5 sets	8 sets	18 sets
Binding	2½″ strips	6	6	9

Continued on page 58.

Frosted Flowers - Facing Page
Ruffled Blanket - Page 73   Pentagon Ball - Page 70

Sleep Tight

BLOCK SIZE: 6″. Photo is of the CRIB size quilt.

Use 42-44″-wide fabric. When strips appear in the cutting list, cut crossgrain strips (selvage to selvage).

	CRIB	CUDDLE	TWIN
Quilt Size	48x60″	54x66″	72x90″
Blocks Set - including setting squares	7x9	8x10	11x14
Total # of Pieced Blocks	32	40	77

Yardage

	CRIB	CUDDLE	TWIN
White-on-white print	2½ yd	3 yd	5 yd
Pastel prints - blocks, binding, border squares	¼ yd each of 11 or more	¼ yd each of 14 or more	¼ yd each of 26 or more
Backing	3¼ yd H	3⅝ yd H	5¾ yd V
Batting	52x64″	60x72″	78x96″

Cutting

White-on-white print		CRIB	CUDDLE	TWIN
Blocks - pieced	2x3½″	128	160	308
Setting squares	6½″ squares	31	40	77
Border	3½″ strips	5	6	8
Bright prints				
Blocks	3½″ squares	3 of each fabric	3 of each fabric	3 of each fabric
	2″ squares	12 of each fabric	12 of each fabric	12 of each fabric
Border	3½″ squares	4 total	4 total	4 total
Binding	2½″ strips	6 total	7 total	9 total

Continued on page 56.

Sleep Tight - Facing Page
Blue or Pink Version - Page 56   Baby Blocks - Page 71

Rubber Ducky

QUILT SIZE: 44x44″
UNIT SIZE: 6″
Use 42-44″-wide fabric. When strips appear in the cutting list, cut crossgrain strips (selvage to selvage). Applique patterns are on insert.

Yardage

Medium blue	lge. star bkg., sm. star center	½ yd
Light blue	sm. star bkg.	⅝ yd
Dark yellow	corner sq., appl.	¼ yd
Medium yellow	sm. star	½ yd
Light yellow	lge. star	½ yd
Blue/yellow print	border	⅝ yd
Applique		
Yellows	ducks	⅙ yd each of 2
Orange	beaks	⅛ yd
White	bubbles	⅛ yd
Binding		½ yd
Backing		3 yd V
Batting		48x48″

Cutting

*Cut these squares in HALF diagonally.

Medium blue	*6⅞″ squares	*10
Light blue	*6⅞″ squares	*4
	6½″ squares	8
Dark yellow	4½″ squares	4
	mama duck	1
Medium yellow	*6⅞″ squares	*6
Light yellow	*6⅞″ squares	*8
Blue/yellow print	4½″ strips	4
Applique	remaining yellow pieces as desired orange beaks, white bubbles	
Binding	2½″ strips	5

Directions

Use ¼″ seam allowance. Diagrams on page 63.

1. HALF-SQUARE TRIANGLE UNITS
   a. Make 16 half-square triangle units with medium blue and light yellow triangles. Press.
   b. Make 8 half-square triangle units with medium yellow and light blue triangles. Press.
   c. Make 4 half-square triangle units with medium yellow and medium blue triangles. Press.
2. ASSEMBLY: Place blocks as shown in diagrams and photo. Stitch into horizontal rows. Stitch rows together. Press.
3. BORDER: Measure length and width of quilt. Cut border strips to the measured length for top, bottom, and side borders. Stitch side borders to quilt. Stitch dark yellow squares to ends of top and bottom borders. Stitch borders to top and bottom of quilt. Press.
4. APPLIQUE: Applique ducks to quilt, referring to diagram and photo. See *Quilting Techniques*, page 11, for fusible web applique directions.
5. Refer to *Finishing Steps for All Quilts*, page 15. Quilt in photo is outline quilted by machine in the star and meander quilted with loops in the border.

Continued on page 63.

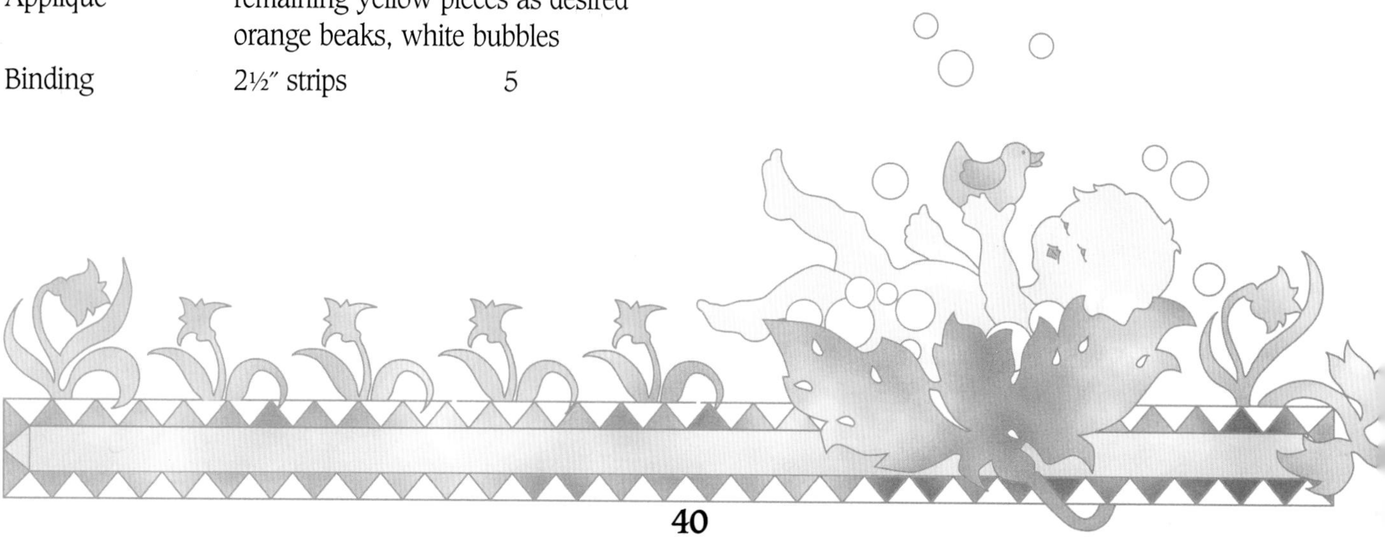

Rubber Ducky - Facing Page

Hooded Cuddler - Page 70   Baby Boxers - Page 74

QUILT SIZE: 48x58″

Use 42-44″-wide fabric. When strips appear in the cutting list, cut crossgrain strips (selvage to selvage). Applique patterns are on insert.

Yardage

Purple	1⅛ yd
Blue (6 fabrics)	⅜ yd each
Red	⅝ yd
Lime green	½ yd
Light blue (2 fabrics)	½ yd each
Yellow (5 fabrics)	⅓ yd each
Teal (2), green print (1)	⅙ yd each
Light purple, medium purple, fuchsia, white	⅛ yd each
Orange (2 fabrics)	⅛ yd each
Binding	⅝ yd
Backing	3¼ yd H
Batting	54x64″

Cutting

Use photo as a guide for fabric placement and diagrams on page 67 as guides for unit numbers/letters.

BORDERS

*Cut these squares in HALF diagonally.

Purple - Border 4	4½″ strips	5
Blue - Border 1	1½″ strips	4
Red - Border 3	*2⅞″ squares	*41
Lime green - Border 2	3″ strips	2
	2½″ strips	3
Light blue - Border 3	*2⅞″ squares	*41
Yellow - Border 3	2½″ squares	4
Border 4	4½″ squares	4

APPLIQUE BACKGROUNDS blue & purple

#1	7½″ square	1
#2	10½x17½″	1
#3	6½x11½″	1
#4, #7, #10	4½″ square	3
#5	10½x18½″	1
#6	8½x6½″	1
#8	8½″ square	1
#9	10½″ square	1

PATCHWORK

Use photo as a guide to color placement.

Patchwork Unit A	2½″ squares	5
Patchwork Unit B	2½″ squares	4 ea. of 2 fab.
Patchwork Unit C	1½ x 4½″	10
Patchwork Unit D	2½ x 4½″	7
	2½″ squares	14
Patchwork Unit E	2½ x 4½″	6
	2½″ squares	12
Patchwork Unit F	*4⅜″ squares	*2 ea. of 2 fab.
Patchwork Unit G	3½″ square	1
	2″ squares	4
	*2⅜″ squares	*4 of bkgr. 4 of foregr.
Patchwork Unit H	2½″ square	1
	2½ x 4½″	4
	*4⅞″ squares	*2
	*2⅞″ squares	*6 of bkgr. 2 of foregr.
Patchwork Unit I	2½ x 4½″	4 of 1st fab. 4 of 2nd fab.
	2½″ squares	4 of 3rd fab. 4 of 4th fab.
APPLIQUE	Use photo, diagrams, & pattern pieces as guides for applique blocks 1-10	
BINDING	2½″ strips	6

Continued on page 66.

Space Dudes - Facing Page
Sunshine & Shadow - Page 52

43

BLOCK SIZE: 12″. Photo is of the CRIB size quilt.
Use 42-44″-wide fabric. When strips appear in the cutting list, cut crossgrain strips (selvage to selvage).

	CRIB	CUDDLE	TWIN
Quilt Size	42x59″	63x63″	69x90″
Blocks Set on Point	2x3	3x3	3x4
Total # of Blocks	6	9	12

Yardage

	CRIB	CUDDLE	TWIN
Dark blue - setting squares & triangles, Border 2	1⅞ yd	2⅜ yd	3⅝ yd
Red - Border 1, binding	¾ yd	1⅛ yd	1⅝ yd
Blue (1), purple (3), green (3), turquoise (1), red (3)	¼ yd each	⅓ yd each	⅜ yd each
Backing	2⅞ yd H	4⅛ yd H	5¾ yd V
Batting	46x63″	69x69″	75x96″

Cutting

*Cut these squares in HALF diagonally.   **Cut these squares in QUARTERS diagonally.

Dark blue				
Setting squares	12½″ squares	2	4	6
Setting triangles - sides	**18¼″ squares	**2	**2	**3
Setting triangles - corners	*9⅜″ squares	*2	*2	*2
Border 2	3½″ strips	5	-	-
	4½″ strips	-	6-7	-
	6½″ strips	-	-	4
	8½″ strips	-	-	4

Red				
Border 1	1½″ strips	5	-	-
	2½″ strips	-	6	-
	3½″ strips	-	-	7
Binding	2½″ strips	6	7	9

BLOCK FABRICS
Use as desired to
cut for each block:

4½″ square	1
*3¾″ squares	*2
*4⅞″ squares	*2
2½″ squares	4 - background
*2⅞″ squares	*8 each of 2 fabrics (1 is background)

Continued on page 60.

Baby Bear Paw - Facing Page
Amish Doll - Page 76

Rockabye

BLOCK SIZE: 4½″. Photo is of the CRIB size quilt.

Use 42-44″-wide fabric. When strips appear in the cutting list, cut crossgrain strips (selvage to selvage).

	CRIB	CUDDLE	TWIN
Quilt Size	47x59″	59x72″	72x89″
Blocks Set on Point before trimming to add borders	7x9	9x11	11x13
Total # of Bar Blocks	48	80	120
Total # of Nine-Patch Blocks	31	49	71
Total # of Setting Squares	32	50	72

Yardage

Cream	1¼ yd	2 yd	2½ yd
Yellow	⅝ yd	⅞ yd	1⅜ yd each
Blue, pink, green, lavender	½ yd each	⅝ yd each	⅞ yd each
Border 1	⅓ yd	⅜ yd	½ yd
Border 2	¾ yd	⅞ yd	1⅜ yd
Binding	⅝ yd	⅝ yd	¾ yd
Backing	3⅛ yd H	3⅞ yd H	5⅝ yd V
Batting	51x63″	65x78″	78x95″

Cutting

Cream				
Setting squares	5″ squares	32	50	72
Blocks	2″ strips	8	12	16
Yellow - blocks	2″ strips	8	13	20
Blue, green, pink,				
lavender - blocks	2″ strips	5 of each fabric	8 of each fabric	12 of each fabric
Border 1	1½″ strips	5	6	8
Border 2	3½″ strips	6	7	4-5
	5½″ strips	-	-	4
Binding	2½″ strips	6	7	9

Continued on page 61.

Rockabye - Facing Page

Bumper Pads - Page 68   Crib Sheet - Page 69   Dust Ruffle - Page 69   Ruffled Blanket - Page 73
Bittersweet Bear pattern available. See page 80 for contacting us.

PHOTO: *Page 21*
QUILT SIZE: 48x56"
SQUARE SIZE: 4"
120 squares set 10x12

Use 42-44"-wide fabric. When strips appear in the cutting list, cut crossgrain strips (selvage to selvage).

Yardage

Pastel prints	⅓ yd each of 12
Pastel mottled solids	⅙ yd each of 4
Border	¾ yd
Binding	⅝ yd
Backing	3¼ yd H
Batting	54x62"

Cutting

Pastel prints	4½" squares	10 of each fabric
Pastel solids	4½" squares	1 of each fabric
Border	4½" strips	5
Binding	2½" strips	6

Directions

Use ¼" seam allowance.

1. ASSEMBLY: Stitch pastel print squares into 12 rows of 10 each. Stitch rows together. Press.

2. BORDER: Measure width and length of quilt. Cut border strips to the measured width for top and bottom borders. Piece border strips to the measured length for side borders. Stitch side borders to quilt. Stitch pastel solid squares to ends of top and bottom borders. Stitch top and bottom borders to quilt. Press.

3. Refer to *Finishing Steps for All Quilts*, page 15. Quilt in photo is meander quilted by machine in the center and straight-line quilted on the border stripe. Small hearts are quilted in the corner border squares.

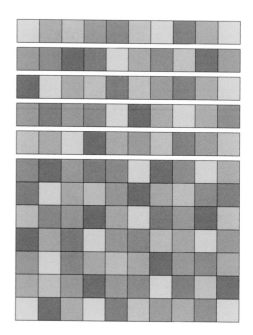

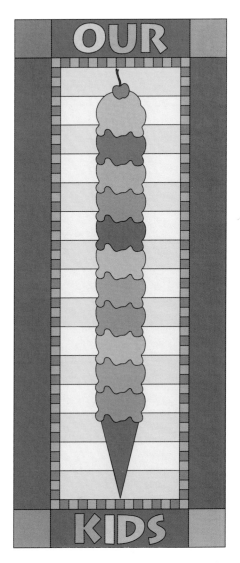

PHOTO: Page 23, on wall. QUILT SIZE: 23 x 55″

Use 42-44″-wide fabric. When strips appear in the cutting list, cut crossgrain strips (selvage to selvage). Applique patterns are on insert.

Yardage

Pastel prints	⅙ yd each of 11
Additional applique	⅙ yd brown for cone
	scraps for cherry & stem
Backgrounds	⅜ yd each of 2
Border 1	⅙ yd each of 2
Border 2	½ yd
Binding	½ yd
Backing	1¾ yd
Batting	27 x 59″

Cutting

Pastel prints		
Ice cream		11
Lettering		as desired
Corner squares	4½″ squares	4
Additional applique	cone, cherry, stem	1 each
Backgrounds	13½ x 3½″	8 of one fabric
		7 of one fabric
Border 1	1½″ strips	3 of each fabric
Border 2	4½″ strips	3
Binding	2½″ strips	5

Directions

Use ¼″ seam allowance.

1. BACKGROUND: Stitch background pieces together, alternating fabrics. Press.

2. BORDER 1: Make 3 strip sets as shown. Press. Crosscut into 1½″ segments. Stitch into 2 side borders and 2 top/bottom borders, referring to diagram. Press. Stitch side borders, then top and bottom borders, to quilt. Press.

3. BORDER 2: Measure width and length of quilt. Cut border strips to the measured width for top and bottom borders. Piece border strips to the measured length for side borders. Stitch side borders to quilt. Stitch corner squares to ends of top and bottom borders. Stitch top and bottom borders to quilt. Press.

4. APPLIQUE: Applique ice cream cone and lettering to quilt. See *Quilting Techniques*, page 11, for fusible web applique directions.

5. Refer to *Finishing Steps for All Quilts*, page 15. Quilt in photo is outline quilted by machine around appliques. Background and Border 1 are ditch quilted. Ice cream cones reduced from applique pattern are quilted in Border 2, and corner squares are quilted with the cherry applique pattern.

6. Hang on wall at desired height. At either side of ice cream cone, use a permanent marker to write kids' names, heights, and the date on the background or on large flat buttons tied to wall hanging with ⅛″ ribbon.

2.

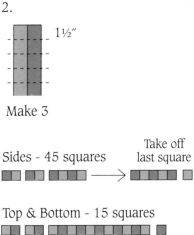

1½″

Make 3

Sides - 45 squares   Take off last square

Top & Bottom - 15 squares

Take off last square

Field of Stars

PHOTO: Page 27
QUILT SIZE: 41 x 66½″
Use 42-44″-wide fabric. When strips appear in the cutting list, cut crossgrain strips (selvage to selvage). Applique pattern is on insert.

Yardage

Blue	2⅛ yd
White	1¼ yd
Binding	⅝ yd
Backing	2⅞ yd H
Batting	47 x 72″

Cutting

Blue - panel	41 x 66½″	1
White	stars	50
Binding	2½″ strips	6

Directions

Use ¼″ seam allowance.

1. Lightly mark right side of panel with horizontal and vertical lines using diagram at right.

2. Applique stars to panel, tilted as shown in diagram, top point on intersections of drawn lines. See *Quilting Techniques*, page 11 for fusible web applique directions.

3. Refer to *Finishing Steps for All Quilts*, page 15. Quilt in photo is meander quilted by machine with stars incorporated into the quilting line.

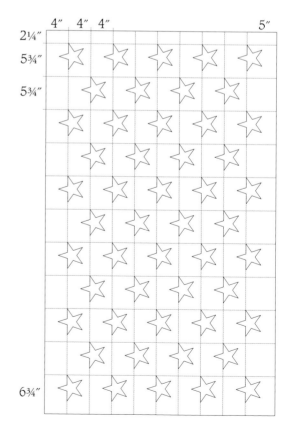

50

Counting Sheep

PHOTO: Page 31, on wall
QUILT SIZE: 38x18″
Use 42-44″-wide fabric. When strips appear in the cutting list, cut crossgrain strips (selvage to selvage). Applique patterns are on insert.

Yardage

Green	grass	⅙ yd each of 2
Blue	sky	⅓ yd
Pink	border	¼ yd
Purple	border	¼ yd
Yellow	numbers	⅛ yd
White	sheep	⅙ yd
Pink	faces, ears	⅛ yd
Brown	legs	⅛ yd
Black	noses	⅛ yd
Plaid	bows	⅛ yd
Binding		⅜ yd
Backing		¾ yd
Batting		42x22″

Cutting

Grass #1	1½x34½″	2
Grass #2	4½x34½″	1
Sky	8½x34½″	1
Border	1½″ strips	4 of each fabric
Appliques	Use photo, diagrams, & pattern pieces as guides	
Binding	2½″ strips	4

Directions

Use ¼″ seam allowance.

1. BACKGROUND: Stitch narrow grass pieces to each side of wide grass piece. Stitch sky to grass unit. Press.
2. BORDER
   a. Make 4 strip sets of 1 purple and 1 pink border strip. Press. Crosscut into 1½″ segments (104 needed).
   b. Make 2 side borders of 14 segments each and 2 top/bottom borders of 38 segments each. See diagram for placement of color.
   c. Stitch side borders to center unit. Stitch top and bottom borders to center unit. Press.
3. APPLIQUE: See *Quilting Techniques*, page 11, for fusible web applique directions.

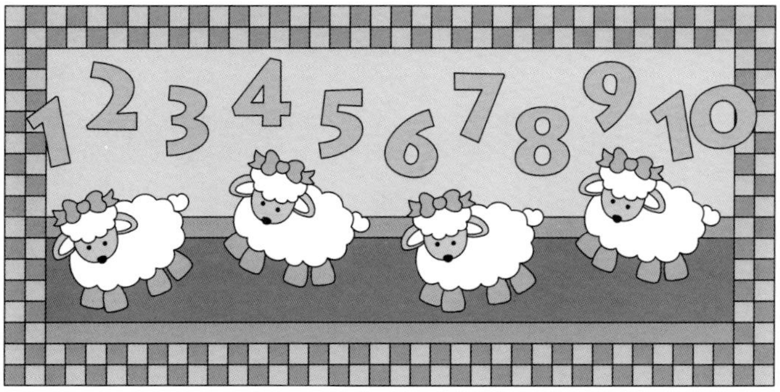

1
2
3
4
5
6
7
8
9
10

4. Refer to *Finishing Steps for All Quilts*, page 15. Quilt in photo is quilted by machine around appliques and in the ditch between grass, sky, and border. Free-motion details such as clouds, grass, fleece lines on sheep, and a wavy line through the center of the border were added. Eyes are small black buttons.

1.

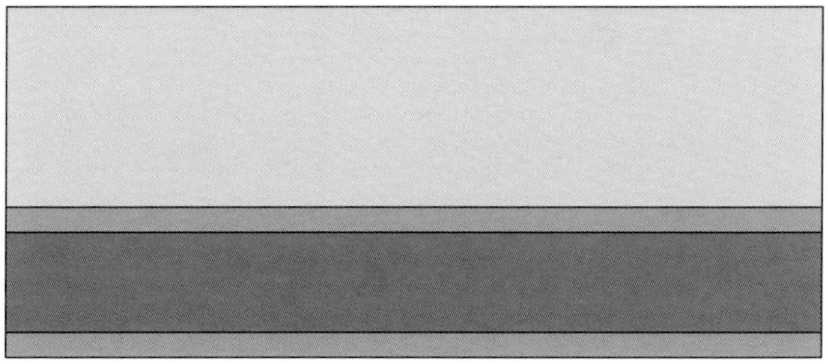

2a.

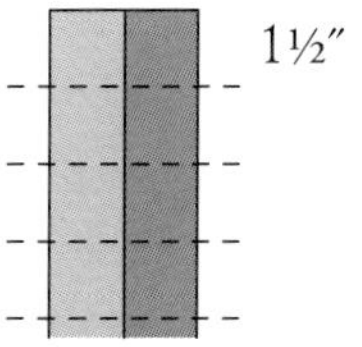

1½″

2b.

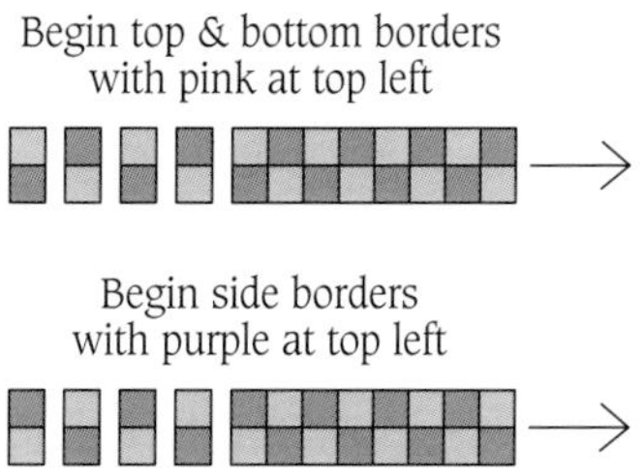

Begin top & bottom borders with pink at top left
Begin side borders with purple at top left

2c.

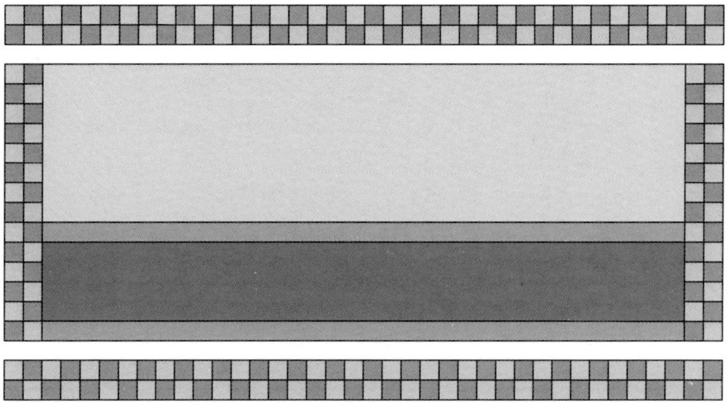

PHOTO: *Page 42*
QUILT SIZE: 44x55″
BLOCK SIZE: 5½″   63 blocks set 7x9

Use 42-44″-wide fabric. When strips appear in the cutting list, cut crossgrain strips (selvage to selvage). Pattern for cutting strip sets is on insert.

Yardage

Black print	1⅜ yd
Bright prints	¼ yd each of 8 fabrics
	2 green, 2 blue, 2 orange, 1 red, 1 yellow
Border	½ yd each of 2 fabrics 1 green, 1 blue
Binding	¼ yd each of 2 fabrics 1 green, 1 blue
Backing	3 yd H
Batting	48x59″

Cutting

*Cut these squares in HALF diagonally.

Black print	*6⅜″ squares	*32
Bright prints	1½″ strips	4 of each fabric
Border	3½″ strips	3 of each fabric
	3½″ squares	1 of each fabric
	*3⅞″ squares	*1 of each fabric
Binding	2½″ strips	3 of each fabric

Directions

Use ¼″ seam allowance.

1. STRIP SETS: Make 4: red/orange/orange/yellow.
   Make 4: blue/blue/green/green. Press.

2. TEMPLATE: Make plastic template of pattern for cutting strip sets (on insert). Line up seam placement lines on seams and cut 8 triangles from each strip set, rotating template as shown.

3. BLOCKS: Stitch triangles cut from strip sets to black triangles. Press. Stack blocks in 4 piles according to rotation of color. Label blue/green piles #1 and #3. Label red/orange/yellow piles #2 and #4.

4. ASSEMBLY: Arrange blocks as shown in 9 rows of 7 each. Stitch rows together. Press.

5. BORDER: Make 2 corner units with triangles cut from 3⅞″ squares. Measure width and length of quilt. Cut border strips to the measured width for top and bottom borders. Piece border strips to the measured length for side borders. Stitch side borders to quilt. Stitch squares and corner units to ends of top and bottom borders. Stitch top and bottom borders to quilt. Press.

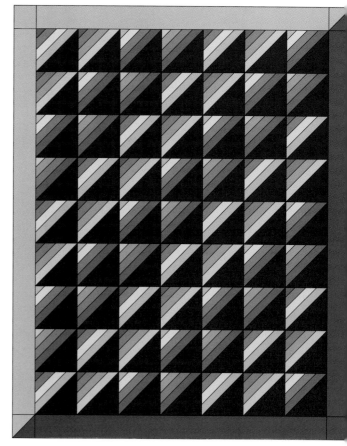

1.

Make 8

2.

Cut 8 from each strip set

3.

Make 63

4.

Top left corner of quilt

1	2	3	4
2	3	4	1
3	4	1	2
4	1	2	3

5.

Make 2

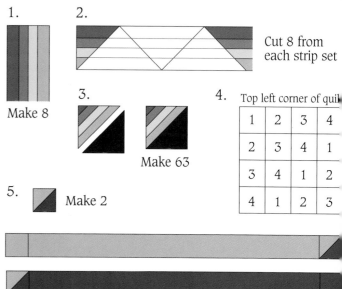

6. Refer to *Finishing Steps for All Quilts*, page 15. Quilt in photo is quilted by machine in the ditch diagonally every other strip, extending into the borders. Binding colors are placed in reverse to border colors with sewn miters at corners where color changes.

Just Ducky

Continued from page 16.

Directions

Use ¼″ seam allowance.

1. BLOCKS: Make blocks following diagram. Press.

2. ASSEMBLY: Stitch blocks into horizontal rows. Stitch rows together. Press.

3. BORDER 1: See *Stairstep Borders*, page 12.

4. BORDERS 2 & 3

   a. Make half-square triangle units. See chart below.

   b. Arrange side borders as shown. Stitch triangle units into rows. Stitch Border 3 pieces together if necessary. Stitch Border 2 to Border 3 for sides. Stitch Border 2/3 units to sides of quilt.

   c. Repeat for top and bottom borders, referring to diagram for corners.

   CRIB 104 half-square triangle units

   22 units per side reversed at center

   24 units across top/bottom plain square at center

   CUDDLE 128 half-square triangle units

   28 units per side reversed at center

   30 units across top/bottom plain square at center

   TWIN 156 half-square triangle units

   38 units per side reversed at center

   34 units across top/bottom plain square at center

5. APPLIQUE: Choose letters and applique name and ducks to top and bottom borders. See *Quilting Techniques*, page 11, for fusible web applique directions.

6. Refer to *Finishing Steps for All Quilts*, page 15.

   Note: Use ¼″ seam allowance to stitch binding to quilt to avoid cutting off points of triangles in Border 3.

   Quilt in photo is machine quilted in the ditch in the block section and in Border 2. Border 3 is quilted with the wave and duck pattern given on the insert. Border 1 and the top section of Border 3 are quilted with reduced versions of the wave pattern given on the insert. Baby ducks, from applique pattern, are quilted in the corner squares of Border 3.

FOR CRIB SIZE:

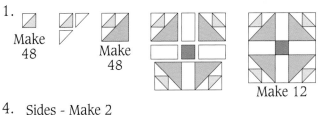

1. Make 48   Make 48   Make 12

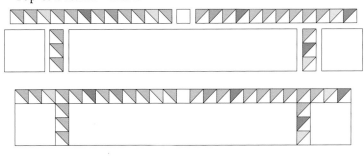

4. Sides - Make 2

Top & Bottom - Make 2

Pretty Posies

Continued from page 20.

Directions

Use ¼″ seam allowance.

1. BLOCKS: Stitch pastel print triangles to opposite sides of white square, then to remaining sides. Press.

2. ASSEMBLY

   a. Arrange blocks in rows. See chart for setting of blocks for your quilt.

   b. Stitch blocks into horizontal rows. Press.

   c. Stitch rows together. Press.

3. BORDERS 1 & 2: See *Stairstep Borders*, page 12.

4. Refer to *Finishing Steps for All Quilts*, page 15. Quilt in photo is quilted by machine in wavy lines on the pastel prints. Small flowers are quilted in the white squares, and a feathered vine is quilted in the white border.

TWIN SIZE

1.

Baby Steps

Continued from page 32.

Directions

Use ¼" seam allowance.

1. UNIT A: Stitch green and blue strips into sets. Press. Crosscut into 6½" segments.
   CRIB - 3 sets, 18 segments
   CUDDLE - 5 sets, 27 segments
   TWIN - 8 sets, 48 segments

2. UNIT B: Stitch purple and yellow strips into sets. Press. Crosscut into 1½" segments.
   CRIB - 2 sets, 30 segments
   CUDDLE - 2 sets, 54 segments
   TWIN - 4 sets, 96 segments

3. UNIT C, Center Segment: Stitch green, fuchsia, and green strips into sets. Press. Crosscut into 2½" segments.
   CRIB - 1 set, 17 segments
   CUDDLE - 2 sets, 27 segments
   TWIN - 3 sets, 48 segments

   UNIT C, Top and Bottom Segments: Stitch yellow, purple, and blue strips into sets. Press. Crosscut into 2½" segments.
   CRIB - 2 sets, 34 segments
   CUDDLE - 4 sets, 54 segments
   TWIN - 6 sets, 96 segments

   Stitch segments into units as shown.

4. ROWS: Arrange and stitch units into vertical rows. NOTE: For Row 1, orient Unit C with yellow square at top left, and for Row 3 orient Unit C with yellow square at top right. For both Row 1 and Row 3, alternate orientation of Unit B as shown in diagram (right-left-right-left, etc.)
   CRIB
   3 Row 1 - A-B-C-B-A-B-C-B-A-B-C-B-A
   2 Row 2 - 8 green & 8 purple squares
   2 Row 3 - C-B-A-B-C-B-A-B-C-B-A-B-C
   CUDDLE
   3 Row 1 - A-B-C-B-A-B-C-B-A-B-C-B-A-B-C-B-A-B
   2 Row 2 - 11 green & 10 purple squares
   3 Row 3 - C-B-A-B-C-B-A-B-C-B-A-B-C-B-A-B-C-B
   TWIN
   4 Row 1 - A-B-C-B-A-B-C-B-A-B-C-B-A-B-C-B-A-
       B-C-B-A-B-C-B
   3 Row 2 - 14 green & 14 purple squares
   4 Row 3 - C-B-A-B-C-B-A-B-C-B-A-B-C-B-A-B-C-B-
       A-B-C-B-A-B

5. ASSEMBLY: Arrange and stitch rows in order:
   Crib - Rows left to right: 1-2-3-1-3-2-1
   Cuddle - Rows left to right: 1-2-3-1-3-2-1-3
   Twin - Rows left to right: 1-2-3-1-3-2-1-3-1-2-3

FOR CRIB SIZE:

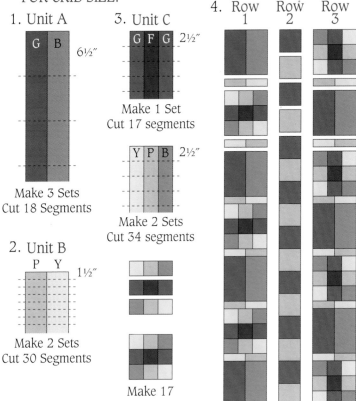

1. Unit A
   G B   6½"
   Make 3 Sets
   Cut 18 Segments

2. Unit B
   P Y   1½"
   Make 2 Sets
   Cut 30 Segments

3. Unit C
   G F G   2½"
   Make 1 Set
   Cut 17 segments

   Y P B   2½"
   Make 2 Sets
   Cut 34 segments

   Make 17

4. Row 1   Row 2   Row 3

6. BORDERS: See *Stairstep Borders*, page 12.

7. Refer to *Finishing Steps for All Quilts*, page 15. Quilt in photo is meander quilted by machine.

Sleep Tight

Continued from page 38.

Directions

Use ¼″ seam allowance.

1. BLOCKS: Make blocks following diagram. Press.

2. ASSEMBLY

   a. Arrange pieced blocks in rows alternating with setting squares. See chart for setting of blocks for your quilt.

   b. Stitch blocks into horizontal rows. Press.

   c. Stitch rows together. Press.

3. BORDER: Measure width and length of quilt. Cut or piece border strips to the measured width for top and bottom borders. Piece border strips to the measured length for side borders.

   Optional: Embroider poem in border.

   Stitch side borders to quilt. Stitch corner squares to ends of top and bottom borders. Stitch top and bottom borders to quilt. Press.

4. Refer to *Finishing Steps for All Quilts*, page 15. Quilt in photo is quilted by machine with straight diagonal lines through the patchwork. Butterflies and hearts are quilted in the setting squares. Wavy lines are quilted in the border.

   Binding: Cut binding strips into 3-5 segments each. Stitch together end to end, randomizing color. Bind.

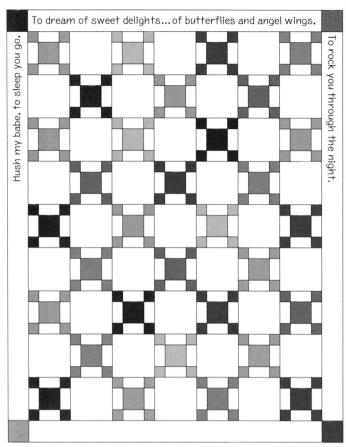

To dream of sweet delights...of butterflies and angel wings.

Hush my babe, to sleep you go.

To rock you through the night.

CRIB SIZE

1.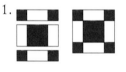

Blue or Pink Version

		CRIB	CUDDLE	TWIN
Quilt Size		48x60″	54x66″	72x90″
Blocks Set - including setting squares		7x9	8x10	11x14
Total # of Pieced Blocks		32	40	77
Yardage				
White print		2⅝ yd	3 yd	4⅞ yd
Blue or pink prints		⅝ yd each of 4	⅝ yd each of 4	⅞ yd each of 4
Backing		3¼ yd H	3⅝ yd H	5¾ yd V
Batting		52x64″	60x72″	78x96″
Cutting				
White print				
Blocks - pieced	2 x 3½″	128	160	308
Setting squares	6½″ squares	31	40	77
Border	3½″ squares	4	4	4
Binding	2½″ strips	6	7	9
Blue or pink prints				
Blocks	3½″ squares	8 of each fabric	10 of each fabric	20 of each fabric
	2″ squares	32 of each fabric	40 of each fabric	77 of each fabric
Border	3½″ strips	1-2 of each fabric	2 of each fabric	2-3 of each fabric

Fish Frenzy

Continued from page 24.

Directions   Use ¼″ seam allowance.

1. BLOCKS: Make number of half-square triangle units listed below with black on one side and light and medium monotones on the other. Make blocks following diagram. Note that black triangles all face the same direction. See top of chart on page 24 for number of blocks to make. Press.

   CRIB - 250   CUDDLE - 494   TWIN - 818

2. APPLIQUE: Applique blocks with starfish and fish, noting which corner is the top of the block. See diagrams for each size quilt at right and below. Refer to *Quilting Techniques*, page 11, for fusible web applique directions. Use permanent markers, embroidery, or paint for faces.

3. SETTING TRIANGLE UNITS FOR SIDES OF QUILT: Stitch sets of 5 and 6 half-square triangle units together for each large side triangle. Note direction of seams and placement of black in each. Units for left and right sides are different. See diagrams. Remove stitching in 2 extending units as shown. Stitch to large triangle. Press.

   CRIB - 3 L, 3 R   CUDDLE - 4 L, 4 R   TWIN - 5 L, 5 R

4. SETTING TRIANGLE UNITS FOR TOP & BOTTOM OF QUILT: Repeat Step 3 but alter the direction of the seams in the half-square triangle units. Units for top and bottom are different. See diagram. Trim extending units leaving ¼″ seam allowance, as shown. Press.

   CRIB - 2 T, 2 B   CUDDLE - 3 T, 3 B   TWIN - 4 T, 4 B

5. ASSEMBLY: Arrange blocks and setting triangle units in diagonal rows, making sure seams in half square triangle units all line up in the same direction. See diagrams for each size at right and below. Stitch blocks into rows. Stitch rows together. Press.

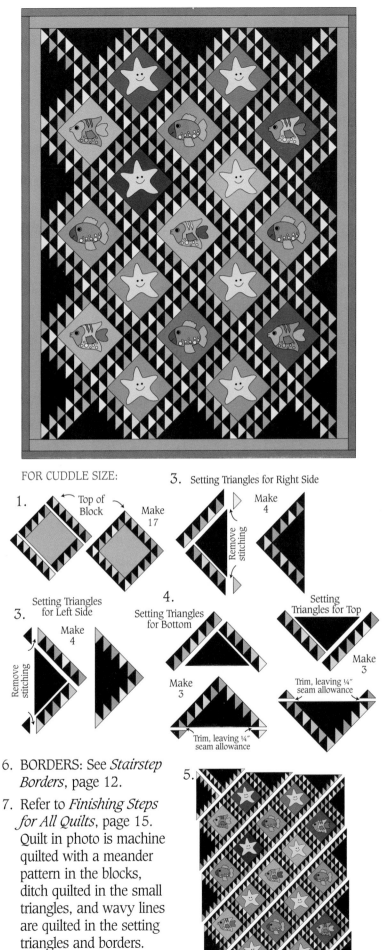

FOR CUDDLE SIZE:

1. Top of Block — Make 17

3. Setting Triangles for Right Side — Remove stitching — Make 4

3. Setting Triangles for Left Side — Remove stitching — Make 4

4. Setting Triangles for Bottom — Make 3 — Trim, leaving ¼″ seam allowance

Setting Triangles for Top — Make 3 — Trim, leaving ¼″ seam allowance

5.

6. BORDERS: See *Stairstep Borders*, page 12.

7. Refer to *Finishing Steps for All Quilts*, page 15. Quilt in photo is machine quilted with a meander pattern in the blocks, ditch quilted in the small triangles, and wavy lines are quilted in the setting triangles and borders.

CRIB SIZE

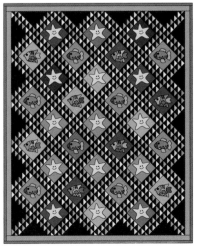

TWIN SIZE

Frosted Flowers

Continued from page 36.

Directions

Use ¼″ seam allowance.

1. BLOCKS: Make number of half-square triangle units listed below, mixing fabrics. Make blocks following diagram. Seams in half-square triangle units must all line up. See top of chart on page 36 for number of blocks to make. Press. Set aside remaining units.

   CRIB - 168   CUDDLE - 250   TWIN - 494

2. APPLIQUE: Applique blocks with flowers, referring to *Quilting Techniques*, page 11, for fusible web applique directions.

3. SETTING TRIANGLE UNITS FOR SIDES OF QUILT: Stitch sets of 5 and 6 triangle units together for each side setting triangle. Note direction of seams in each. See diagram. Remove stitching in 2 extending units as shown. Stitch to large triangle. Press.

   CRIB - Make 2   CUDDLE - Make 4   TWIN - Make 6

4. SETTING TRIANGLE UNITS FOR TOP & BOTTOM OF QUILT: Repeat Step 3 but alter the direction of the seams in the triangle units. See diagram. Stitch to large triangle, then trim extending units leaving ¼″ seam allowance, as shown. Press.

   CRIB - Make 2   CUDDLE - Make 2   TWIN - Make 4

5. SETTING TRIANGLE UNITS FOR CORNERS: Stitch 2 sets of 6 triangle units together noting direction of seams. See diagram. Remove stitching in one extending unit as shown. Stitch to corner triangles. Trim other extending unit as shown. Press. Make 2 for top left and bottom right of quilt. Repeat directions, altering direction of seams, to make top right and bottom left corner units.

6. ASSEMBLY: Arrange blocks and setting triangle units in diagonal rows, making sure seams in half square triangle units are placed vertically. See top of chart on page 36 for number of blocks across and down. For Cuddle and Twin sizes, start as shown at right and add blocks to right and down. For Cuddle (and Twin) quilts, place 4 (8) blocks with same background in center of quilt. Stitch blocks into rows. Stitch rows together. Press.

7. BORDERS: See *Mitered Borders*, page 12.

8. Refer to *Finishing Steps for All Quilts*, page 15. Quilt in photo is machine quilted in a meander pattern in the backgrounds and ditch quilted in the half-square triangle units. Modified versions of the applique pattern are quilted in the setting triangles. Wavy lines are quilted in Borders 1 and 2, and a flower/butterfly motif is quilted in Border 3.

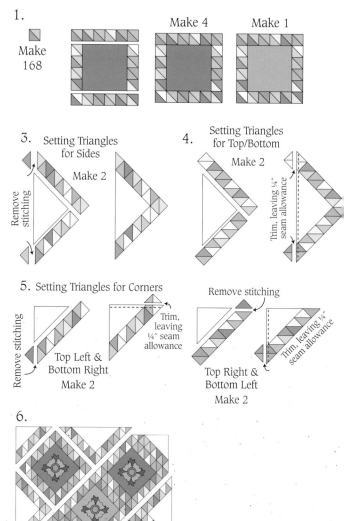

FOR CRIB SIZE:

1.
Make 168   Make 4   Make 1

3. Setting Triangles for Sides
Make 2
Remove stitching

4. Setting Triangles for Top/Bottom
Make 2
Trim, leaving ¼″ seam allowance

5. Setting Triangles for Corners
Remove stitching
Top Left & Bottom Right
Make 2
Trim, leaving ¼″ seam allowance

Remove stitching
Top Right & Bottom Left
Make 2
Trim, leaving ¼″ seam allowance

6.

Sweet Dreams

continued from page 34.

Directions

Use ¼″ seam allowance.

1. PINWHEEL BLOCKS: Make blocks following diagram. See top of chart on page 34 for number to make. Press.

2. NINE-PATCH UNITS & FOUR-PATCH BLOCKS

   a. Make strip sets following diagram. Press.

      CRIB - 2 Set A, 1 Set B
      CUDDLE - 3 Set A, 2 Set B
      TWIN - 5 Set A, 3 Set B

   b. Crosscut strip sets into 2″ segments.

   c. Stitch segments into units as shown. Press.

      CRIB - 20
      CUDDLE - 30
      TWIN - 48

   d. Stitch Nine-Patch units and yellow 5″ squares into Four-Patch blocks as shown. See top of chart on page 34 for number to make. Press.

3. ASSEMBLY: Starting with a pinwheel block in the upper left corner, arrange blocks alternately. See top of chart on page 34 for number across and down. Stitch blocks into horizontal rows. Stitch rows together. Press.

4. BORDER 1: See *Stairstep Borders*, page 12.

   CRIB - 1½″ strips for sides, 2″ strips for top/bottom
   CUDDLE - 2″ strips for sides, 2½″ strips for top/btm.
   TWIN - 3½″ strips for sides & top/bottom

5. BORDER 2: Make half-square triangle units and stitch into borders in chart below. Stitch side borders to quilt. See whole-quilt diagram for orientation. Stitch 2″ green squares to ends of top/bottom borders and stitch borders to quilt.

   CRIB - 24 units for sides, 19 units for top/bottom
   CUDDLE - 29 units for sides, 24 units for top/btm.
   TWIN - 39 units for sides, 30 units for top/bottom

6. BORDER 3: See *Stairstep Borders*, page 12.

7. Refer to *Finishing Steps for All Quilts*, page 15. Quilt in photo is meander quilted by machine in the background areas and echo quilted in the pinwheel blocks. Straight lines are quilted diagonally across the Nine-Patch units. Border 1 is quilted with a wavy line, Border 2 is ditch quilted, and Border 3 is quilted with a leaf pattern.

FOR CRIB SIZE:

1.

Make 40

Make 10

2.

Set A Make 2   Set B Make 1

Make 20

Make 10

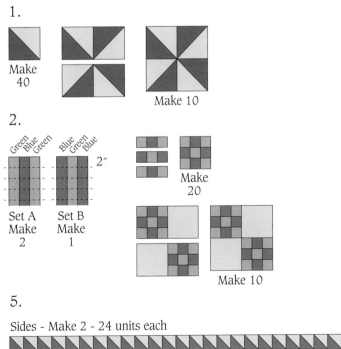

5.

Sides - Make 2 - 24 units each

Top & Bottom - Make 2 - 19 units each

Baby Bear Paw

Continued from page 44.

Directions

Use ¼″ seam allowance.

1. BLOCKS: Make blocks following diagram. See top of chart on page 44 for number of blocks to make. Press.

2. ASSEMBLY: Arrange blocks, setting squares, and setting triangles in diagonal rows. See top of chart on page 44 for number of blocks across and down. Stitch blocks into rows. Stitch rows together. Press.

3. BORDERS: See *Stairstep Borders*, page 12.

4. Refer to *Finishing Steps for All Quilts*, page 15. Quilt in photo is machine quilted in the ditch in the blocks. Simple flower and feather wreaths are quilted in the centers of the blocks and in the setting triangles. A cable with hearts in the corners is quilted in Border 2.

1.   For each block:

Make 16   Make 4   Make 2

CRIB SIZE

2.

60

Rockabye

Continued from page 46.

Directions

Use ¼″ seam allowance.

1. BAR BLOCKS
   CRIB - 3 Set A, 3 Set B - 24 segments each
   CUDDLE - 5 Set A, 5 Set B - 40 segments each
   TWIN - 8 Set A, 8 Set B - 60 segments each

2. NINE-PATCH BLOCKS
   CRIB - 2 each Set C, D, E - 31 segments each
   CUDDLE - 3 each Set C, D, E - 49 segments each
   TWIN - 4 each Set C, D, E - 71 segments each

3. ASSEMBLY

   a. Arrange blocks and setting squares in diagonal rows following diagram for placement of blocks and color. *Color placement is critical to getting the woven look of this quilt.* Begin all 3 sizes of quilts in the same way, at the top left corner.

   b. Count the on-point nine-patch blocks and setting squares at outside edge:

      CRIB - 7 x 9
      CUDDLE - 9 x 11
      TWIN - 11 x 13

   c. Stitch blocks together in diagonal rows. Stitch rows together. Press.

   d. Trim outside edge of quilt, leaving ¼″ seam allowance.

4. BORDERS 1 & 2: See *Stairstep Borders*, page 12. For twin size, 5½″ border strips are for top/bottom borders, 3½″ border strips are for side borders.

5. Refer to *Finishing Steps for All Quilts*, page 15. Quilt in photo is quilted by machine with wavy lines on the pastel prints and Border 1. Flowers are quilted in the cream setting squares. Border 2 is quilted around the flowers in the print.

FOR CRIB SIZE

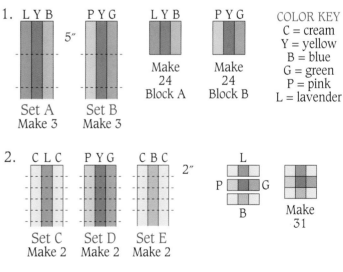

1. L Y B   P Y G   L Y B   P Y G   COLOR KEY
   5″   C = cream
                     Make   Make   Y = yellow
                     24   24   B = blue
                     Block A Block B G = green
   Set A   Set B   P = pink
   Make 3 Make 3   L = lavender

2. C L C   P Y G   C B C   2″   L
                                     P   G
                                       B
   Set C   Set D   Set E   Make
   Make 2 Make 2 Make 2   31

3a-c.

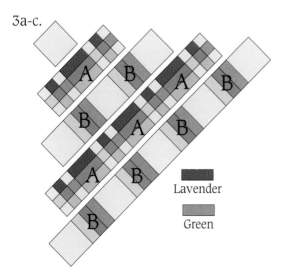

A B A B
B A A B
A B
B

Lavender

Green

3d.

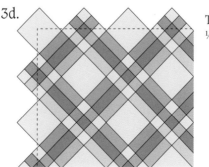

Trim, leaving ¼″ seam allowance

61

ABCs & 123s

Continued from page 18.

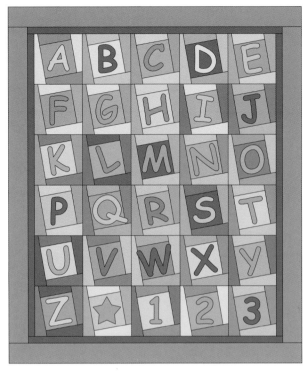

1b.

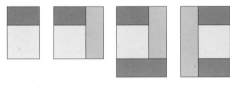

1d.

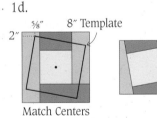

⅝"   8" Template

2"

Match Centers

Sweet Hearts

Continued from page 28.

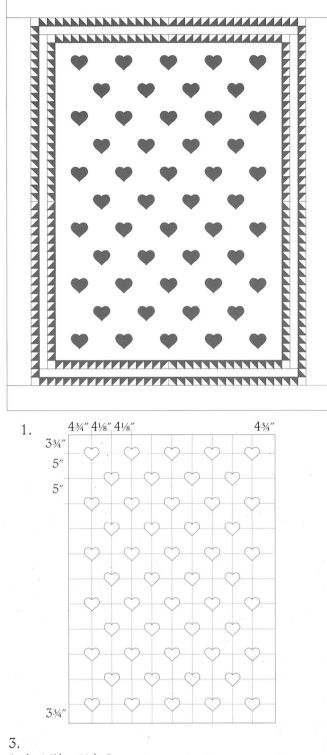

1. 4¾" 4⅛" 4⅛"   4¾"

3¾"

5"

5"

3¾"

3.

Border 1 Sides - Make 2

Border 1 Top & Bottom - Make 2

5.

Border 3 Sides - Make 2

Border 3 Top & Bottom - Make 2

62

Forever Stripes

continued from page 26.

Rubber Ducky

Continued from page 40.

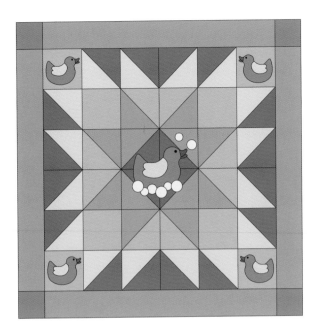

1.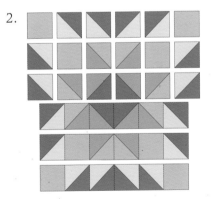

Make 16	Make 8	Make 4
Lt. Yellow & med. blue	Med yellow & lt. blue	Med. yellow & med. blue

2.

3.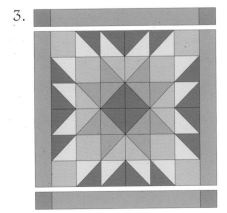

Snuggle Up

Continued from page 22.

3.

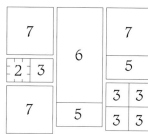
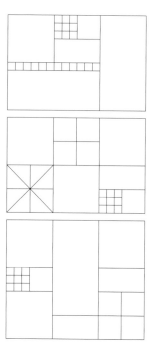
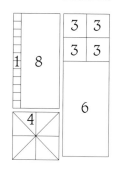

1.

Unit 1

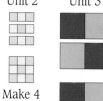

Make 2

Unit 2

Make 4

Unit 3

Make 4

Unit 4

Make 3

Fuzzy Wuzzy

Continued from page 30.

5. BORDER: Measure width and length of quilt. Piece border strips to the measured length for side borders. Stitch side borders to quilt. Cut or piece border strips to the measured length for top and bottom borders. Stitch corner squares to ends. Stitch top and bottom borders to quilt. Press.

6. Refer to *Finishing Steps for All Quilts*, page 15. Quilt in photo is machine quilted in the ditch in the center panel, outline quilted in center panel background, and two straight parallel lines are quilted in border.

7. Wash and dry quilt to fringe raw edges.

1.

STACK:
Lge. plaid
Sm. purple
Sm. pink

Make 18

STACK:
Lge. yellow
Sm. pink
Sm. purple

Make 58

2. Set A   Set B

4½″

Make 3   Make 3

Make 24

3a.

Make 10

Make 7

4.

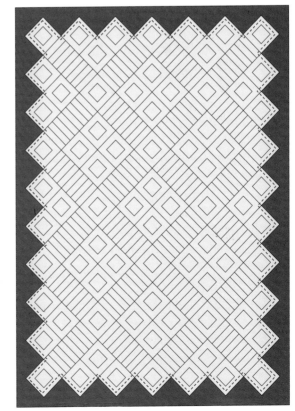

3b.

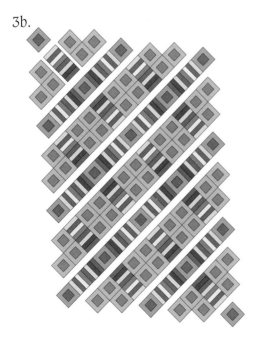

Space Dudes

Continued from page 42.

Directions

Use ¼″ seam allowance.

NOTE: As blocks are made, use paint or permanent marker for eyeballs, noses, mouths, and topknot. Embroider the yo-yo string. After quilting, stitch buttons to quilt for stars in Block 1, body detail in Block 9, and foot detail in Block 8.

1. PATCHWORK UNITS: Make units shown in diagrams on page 67. For Units D, E, and I, place 2½″ square right sides together on end of 2½ x 4½″ rectangle. Mark across square diagonally with a pencil. Stitch on line. Trim seam allowance to ¼″. Press.

2. APPLIQUE UNITS: Refer to diagram and photo for applique units including corner squares for Border 4. Keep appliques out of seam allowance. Leave arms in Unit 3, tail and topknot in Unit 6, and head in Unit 8 unpressed and unstitched until units have been stitched together. See *Quilting Techniques*, page 11, for fusible web applique directions.

3. ASSEMBLY: Stitch units into panels as shown in diagram. Stitch panels together. Press. Finish applique.

4. BORDER 1: See *Stairstep Borders*, page 12.

5. BORDER 2: Measure length of quilt. Cut or piece 2½″ border strips to the measured length. Stitch to sides of quilt. Repeat with 3″ strips for top and bottom borders. Press.

6. BORDER 3: Make 82 half-square triangle units. Stitch into borders as shown in diagram. Stitch side borders to quilt. Stitch yellow squares to ends of top and bottom borders. Stitch borders to top and bottom of quilt. Press.

7. BORDER 4: Measure length and width of quilt. Piece side borders and stitch to quilt. Cut border strips for top and bottom borders. Stitch yellow squares to ends. Stitch borders to top and bottom of quilt. Press.

8. Refer to *Finishing Steps for All Quilts*, page 15. Quilt in photo is outline and ditch quilted by machine in the center panel. Border 2 is outline quilted, Border 3 is ditch quilted, and Border 4 is quilted with a loop-de-loop and stars pattern.

1.

A — 2x10" Finished Size

B — 4" Fin.

C — 4x10" Finished Size

D — 4 x14" Finished Size

E — 4x12" Finished Size

F — 7" Finished

G — 6" Finished

H — 10" Finished

I — 8" Finished

3.

6.

Sides - Make 2 - 23 units each

Top & Bottom - Make 2 - 18 units each

Pentagon Balls

Photos on pages 19, 23, 70
4½″ and 7″ diameter

Fabric & Supplies

Fabric scraps at least 4″ or 6″ square - 12
Stuffing

Cutting

12 pentagons for each block - patterns below

Directions

Use ¼″ seam allowance.

1. TWO HALVES: Stitch 6 pentagons together in numerical sequence following diagram, beginning and ending stitching ¼″ from each edge. Make 2.

2. ASSEMBLE: Matching peaks to valleys, stitch 2 halves together, leaving one edge open for stuffing.

3. STUFF: Turn; stuff firmly. Fold raw edges in and whipstitch opening closed.

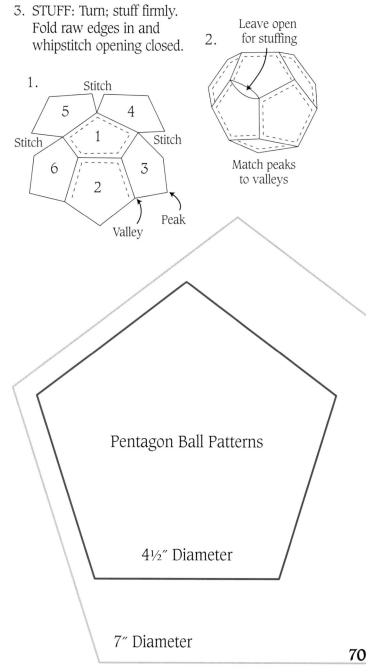

Pentagon Ball Patterns

4½″ Diameter

7″ Diameter

Hooded Cuddler

Photos on pages 31, 41

Yardage & Supplies

Polar fleece or terry cloth	1 yd	
Cotton print for bias trim	⅓ yd	
½-⅝″ ribbon	1 yd	

Cutting

Fleece or terry cloth	33″ square
Bias trim fabric	10-11 bias strips 2″ wide

Directions

1. BIAS: Stitch bias strips together end to end, right sides together. Press seams open. Press in half lengthwise wrong sides together. Open out. Press ¼″ to wrong side on each long edge.

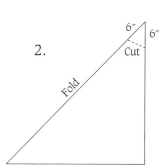

2. CASING: Fold square in half diagonally. Cut off 6″ tip as shown. Lay square right side up and draw a curved casing line for hood. See diagram. Open out center fold of bias strip and pin strip along line, ends folded under and ending ½″ from center front. Stitch close to each long folded edge, leaving ends open for ribbon.

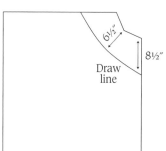

3. HOOD SEAM: Fold cuddler right sides together and stitch seam at top of hood. Zigzag raw edges of seam.

4. BIAS TRIM: Trim remaining three corners so they are rounded. Mark around a saucer or use a compass to make a pattern. Enclose outside edge of cuddler with folded bias and topstitch through all layers.

5. RIBBON: Insert ribbon through casing and tie knots in ends.

Baby Blocks

Photos on pages 19, 31, 39
4"

Fabric & Supplies - for one block

Fabric scraps at least 5" square	6 for block
Foam cube	1 piece 3¾"
6-oz polyester batting	1 piece 4 x 16"
	2 pieces 4 x 4"
Optional: Clear vinyl .4 mil thick	1 piece 4½ x 4"
Optional: fabric scraps for applique	

Cutting

6 squares 4½" for each block
Optional applique - use 3" letters from insert
  and/or small heart and star

Directions

Use ¼" seam allowance.

1. OPTIONAL PHOTO POCKET: Place vinyl on right side of one square, matching 3 edges. Baste together along 3 edges in the seam allowance.

2. OPTIONAL APPLIQUE: Machine applique letters and/or heart and star to right side of each square, centered. See *Quilting Techniques*, page 11, for fusible web applique directions.

3. ASSEMBLE

   a. Place all squares following diagram in right-reading position (alphabet letters right side up and readable). Stitch squares together in numerical sequence following diagram, beginning and ending stitching ¼" from each edge. Be careful not to catch open side of vinyl window in stitching. Leave edges without numbers unstitched for inserting foam.

   b. Turn right side out. Wrap 4 x 16" piece of batting around foam cube and whipstitch ends together. Whipstitch 4" squares to remaining sides.

   c. Insert batting-covered foam cube into fabric covering. Whipstitch remaining three edges of block closed.

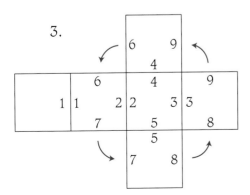

Bib

Photo on page 17

Yardage

Bib fabric	⅜ yd
Bias trim fabric	⅓ yd

Cutting

Bib fabric	1 rectangle 10½ x 13"
	1 rectangle 10½ x 4"
Trim fabric	6-7 bias strips 2" wide

Directions

1. CUT: Trim all corners of large rectangle and 2 corners of small rectangle so they are rounded. Mark around a cup or saucer or use a compass to make a pattern. See diagram. Using a 5" saucer or paper pattern, mark and cut out neck opening on one short side of large rectangle.

2. BIAS: Stitch bias strips end to end, right sides together. Press seams open. Press in half lengthwise, wrong sides together. Open out. Press each long edge to the middle, making ½" double-folded bias.

3. ENCLOSE EDGES: Enclose straight edge of pocket with folded bias and stitch (a serpentine stitch works well for this) in place. Pin or baste pocket to bottom edge of bib. Enclose all but neck edge of bib with folded bias.

4. TIE: Cut a 42" length of bias for neck edge/tie. Mark center of bias and center of neck edge. Matching centers, pin bias to neck edge, enclosing raw edge. Stitch in place from one end of tie, along neck edge, to other end of tie. Make overhand knots in ends of tie, if desired.

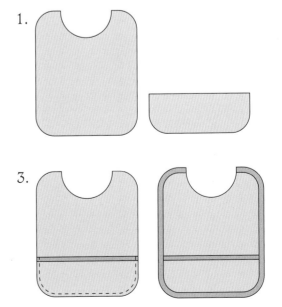

Instant High Chair

Photo on page 17
Make pattern from grid diagram at right.

Yardage & Supplies

Front	¾ yd
Back & ties	1 yd
¾" elastic	14" piece
Thin cotton batting	24 x 36"

Cutting

1 front using pattern
1 back using pattern
2 ties 5 x 40"

Directions

Use ½" seam allowance.

1. FRONT: Place front on batting, wrong side down. Pin baste well. Machine quilt in diagonal lines. Trim batting even with front.

2. TIES: Fold tie pieces in half lengthwise, right sides together. Stitch, leaving one end open. Clip, turn, and press. Stitch ties to narrow end of front between marks, facing in. See diagram. Pin ties to front, away from seam allowances.

3. BACK: Pin back to front, right sides together. Stitch, leaving a 6" opening on wide end for turning. Trim corners and clip curves. Turn right side out and press. Stitch opening closed.

4. CASING: Stitch wide end close to edge. Stitch a parallel line 1" from first stitching. Pop a few stitches of each side seam between lines of casing. Insert elastic between front and back, stitching each end of elastic firmly at side edges. Stitch openings closed.

5. CHAIR POCKET: Fold wide end of instant high chair 4" to back and stitch side edges. See diagram. Fit elasticized pocket over back of chair, put baby in chair, fold narrow end up between baby's legs and tie around chair.

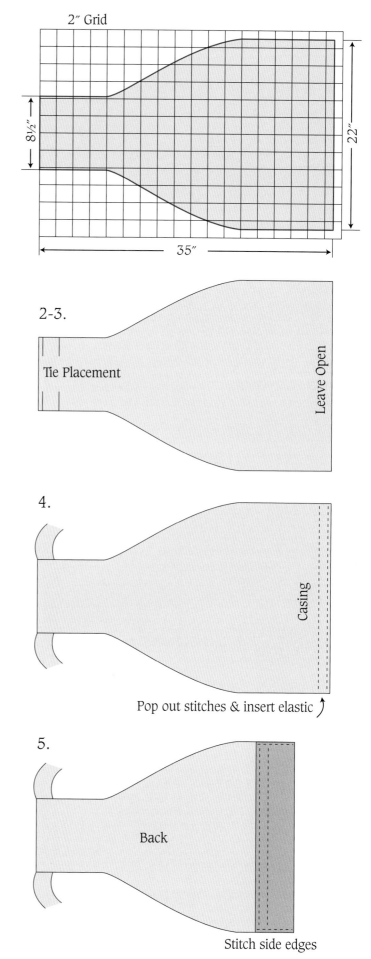

2" Grid

8½"

22"

35"

2-3.

Tie Placement

Leave Open

4.

Casing

Pop out stitches & insert elastic

5.

Back

Stitch side edges

Quilt-in-a-Pillow

NOTE: Use these directions to make any medium-sized quilt into a Quilt-in-a-Pillow.

Yardage & Supplies

Bound quilt, cuddle or crib size
½ "pillow pocket" fabric OR 2 contrasting fabrics
Thin batting

Cutting

2 squares "pillow pocket" fabric:

⅓ the width of the quilt + 3″

For example, for 48″-wide quilt: 16″ + 3″ = 19″

1 piece batting 1″ bigger than fabric squares

Directions

1. PILLOW POCKET: Place two fabric squares right sides together. Center on batting square. Stitch entire outside edge ¼″ from edges of fabric squares, leaving part of one side open for turning. Trim excess batting. Clip corners, turn right side out, and press. Slip stitch opening closed. Quilt square as desired.

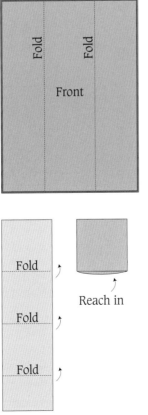

Pocket Opening

Back

2. STITCH: Place quilted square upside down on back of quilt, centered on one end. Side of pillow pocket facing quilt at this point will be facing out when quilt is folded into it. Stitch close to three edges as shown, backstitching at each end of stitching line.

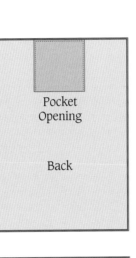

Fold   Fold

Front

3. FOLD: Lay quilt on floor right side up and fold it lengthwise into thirds. Starting at end without pocket, fold into segments the same size as the pocket. Reach into pocket and pull it over the folded quilt.

Fold

Fold

Fold

Reach in

Ruffled Blanket

Photos on pages 35, 37, 47
36x36″
Applique pattern is on insert.

Yardage

Polar fleece - brushed on both sides - 1 yd
   (can also use purchased thermal receiving blanket)
Ruffle fabric   ⅞ yd
Optional applique   scraps at least 5″ square

Cutting

Polar fleece   33″ square
Ruffle fabric   7 strips 3½″ wide
Optional applique   use Frosted Flowers pattern

Directions

1. CUT: Using a cup or small saucer as a pattern, round corners of fleece square.

2. RUFFLE

   a. Stitch ruffle strips end to end.

   b. Hem one long edge with a double-folded ¼″ hem.

   c. Press ⅜″ to wrong side on opposite long edge.

   d. Using a ruffler set for 2 to 1 fullness, ruffle pressed edge of fabric strip.

   e. With edges overlapped ⅜″, pin ruffle, wrong side down, on right side of fleece square. Trim ends where they meet, leaving ⅜″ seam allowance on each.

   f. Topstitch ruffle to fleece square. Where ends meet, turn under one end of ruffle and topstitch in place.

3. OPTIONAL APPLIQUE: Applique flower in one corner of blanket. Refer to *Quilting Techniques*, page 11, for fusible web applique directions.

Baby Boxers

Photos on pages 17, 19, 35, 41
Size 12-month
Pattern is on insert. Trace onto pattern paper.

Yardage & Supplies

Fabric   ½ yd
1½″ elastic   ¾ yd

Directions

Use ½″ seam allowance.

1. CUT: Fold fabric in half, selvage to selvage. Matching grain line arrow on pattern to lengthwise grain of fabric, pin pattern to fabric. Cut out.

2. INNER LEG SEAM: Stitch inner leg seam of each piece. Press open.

3. CROTCH SEAM: Pin two boxer legs right sides together, one inside the other, matching waist edges, inner leg seams, and notches. Stitch crotch seam. Stitch again close to first stitching. Clip curve. Press seam allowance open.

4. WAIST CASING

   a. Press ¼″ of waist edge to wrong side. Press waist edge to inside along fold line. Stitch close to lower folded edge, through all layers, leaving a 3″ opening for inserting elastic. Topstitch top edge of casing close to edge.

   b. Cut elastic the measurement of the child's waist plus 1″. Pin a large safety pin to one end of elastic and insert into casing. Pull ends of elastic out of casing, lap ends ½″, and stitch securely.

   c. Push elastic back into casing and topstitch opening closed.

5. HEM: To hem leg openings, turn a ¼″ double hem to inside and stitch next to fold.

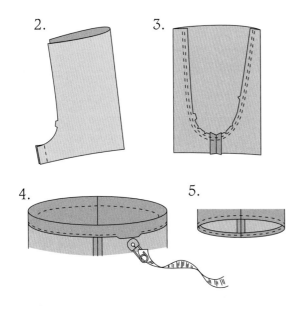

Beanbag Game Board

Photo on page 25

Yardage & Supplies

2 coordinating fabrics   ⅔ yd each
Black   ⅔ yd
Foamcore   36″ square
Wide packing tape

Cutting

4 squares 10½″ of first coordinating fabric
5 squares 10½″ of second coordinating fabric
2 pieces 6 x 30½″ of black
2 pieces 6 x 35¾″ of black

Directions

Use ¼″ seam allowance.

1. MAKE FABRIC TOP: Stitch squares together as shown. Press. Stitch short black pieces to sides. Stitch long black pieces to top and bottom. Press.

2. ASSEMBLE: Place fabric top right side down on floor. Center foamcore on top. Pull opposite sides snugly to back of foamcore and tape in place. Pull remaining opposite sides to back and tape.

3. GAMES: Play Tic-Tac-Toe using beanbags below. Let the kids make up original games of their own.

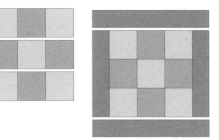

Fish Frenzy Beanbags

Photo on page 25. Patterns & more directions are on insert.

Fabric & Supplies for 5 fish & 5 starfish

Polar fleece - ⅓ yd yellow, ⅓ yd green, ⅛ yd blue
Buttons for eyes - 10 blue ⅝″, 10 black ⅜″
Filler beads, rice, or beans

Directions

1. CUT: Starfish - 5 & 5 reversed (yellow). Fish - 5 bodies & 5 bodies reversed (green), 5 each of fins and tail (blue).

2. STITCH: Stitch eyes on right side of 5 starfish. Stitch 1 eye on each fish shape, 5 facing right and 5 facing left. Place 2 shapes together and stitch around shape ¼″ from edge, leaving open for stuffing. Sandwich fins and tail between fish pieces and catch them in stitching. Do not turn. Fill. Stitch openings closed.

Crib Organizer

Photo on page 33
22 x 22″

Yardage

Background, border, binding	1⅛ yd
Pockets	⅝ yd
Pocket binding, ties, backing	1½ yd
Batting	26 x 26″

Cutting

Background	20½″ square
Border	3 strips 1½″ wide
Binding	3 strips 2½″ wide
Pockets	32½ x 9½″ - upper
	26½ x 8½″ - lower
Pocket binding	2 strips 2½″ wide
Ties	3 pieces 3½ x 32½″
Backing	26″ square

Directions

Use ¼″ seam allowance.

1. PREPARE POCKETS: Bind top edges of pockets. Press ½″ to wrong side on lower edge of upper pocket.

2. PLEAT POCKETS: Measure, mark, fold, and press pockets as shown, leaving ¼″ seam allowance at each side.

3. FINISH LOWER POCKET: Fold background square in half and crease center. Place lower pocket on background, matching centers, side edges, and lower edges. Stitch pocket to backing on center line, reinforcing at bound edge of pocket. Pin or baste lower edge and sides of pocket to background, keeping folds of side pleats out of seam allowance.

4. FINISH UPPER POCKET: Pin upper pocket to background, 1½″ above lower pocket, binding at top edge; match centers and side edges, keeping folds of side pleats out of seam allowance. Stitch across bottom edge of pocket close to edge. Stitch center line of pocket and center lines of remaining box pleats. Pin or baste side edges of pocket to background, keeping folds of side pleats out of seam allowance.

2. Measure & mark lower pocket

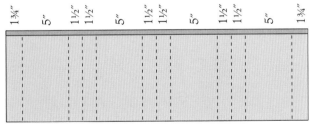

Fold & press

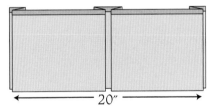

20″

Measure & mark upper pocket

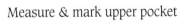

Fold & press

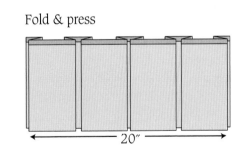

20″

3-4.

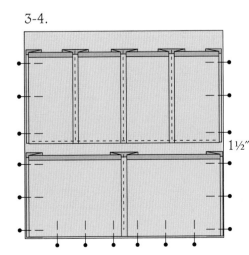

1½″

5. BORDER: See *Stairstep Borders*, page 12. Keep folds of side pleats out of seam allowance.

6. LAYER & QUILT: Refer to *Finishing Steps for all Quilts*, page 15. The crib organizer in the photo was quilted in the ditch between the pockets and the border, along the center line, and along the upper pocket pleat centers.

7. TIES: Fold rectangles for ties in half lengthwise, right sides together. Stitch entire raw edge, leaving a 3″ opening for turning. Clip corners, turn, and press ties. Hand stitch openings closed. Fold ties in half, space evenly across top edge of crib pocket, on the back, and stitch in place along fold.

8. Tie crib organizer to crib rail and fill with toys.

Amish Doll

Photo on page 45
19″ tall

Fabric & Supplies

Fabric	body	⅜ yd muslin or light peach
	dress	⅝ yd navy
	apron	⅓ yd fuchsia
	shoes, pantaloons, bonnet	⅔ yd black
Fusible interfacing		⅙ yd - heavyweight
½″ ribbon		⅔ yd black
Embroidery floss		1 skein ecru or peach
		1 skein black
Fiberfil		1 lb.

Cutting

For the pieces in this section, enlarge patterns from graph on page 77.

Body	2
Arms	2, 2 reversed
Legs	2, 2 reversed
Shoes	2, 2 reversed
Bonnet	2
Dress bodice	2
Apron bodice	2

For the pieces in this section, mark dimensions directly on fabric and cut out.

Pantaloons	2 rectangles 9¼ x 12½″
Bonnet brim	2 rectangles 2½ x 10″
Dress sleeve	2 squares 8″
Dress skirt	1 rectangle 11 x 29″
Apron skirt	1 rectangle 7¼ x 10½″
Apron pocket	1 square 2″
Apron tie	1 rectangle 2 x 29″
Bonnet brim	2 rectangles of interfacing 2½ x 10″

Directions

Use ¼″ seam allowance.

1. DOLL BODY

   a. TRANSFER MARKINGS: Transfer shoulder and lower body markings to right side of body pieces. Transfer dotted lines to right sides of arm and leg pieces. Transfer dots to arm and leg pieces. Transfer dotted line to one dress bodice piece.

   b. BODY/HEAD: Stitch body/head pieces, right sides together, leaving lower edge open between markings. Clip neck curves. Turn right side out.

   c. LEGS: Stitch shoes, right sides together, to ends of legs, matching notches. Make 2, make 2 reversed. Stitch leg/shoe pieces, right sides together, matching shoe seams, leaving open at top. Make 2. Clip at ankles. Turn right side out.

   d. ARMS: Stitch 2 arms right sides together, leaving top edge open. Make 2. Clip at thumb and wrist. Turn right side out.

   e. STUFF ARMS & LEGS: Stuff arms and legs to dotted lines. Tie ecru or peach embroidery floss tightly around arms and legs at dotted lines to create joints. Finish stuffing arms and legs to 1½″ from top.

   f. SHOULDERS: Fold in seam allowance at top of arm. Bring arm seams together then bring dots in to arm seams. Flatten to form pleats. See diagram. Match marked shoulder lines on body and stitch, forming a triangle. Place arms with thumbs facing front on top of shoulder triangles. Stitch through all layers.

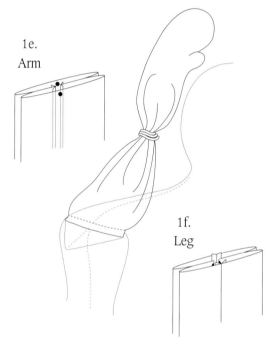

1e.
Arm

1f.
Leg

   g. STUFF BODY: Match seams at tops of legs, pleat, and flatten like arms. Pin legs feet forward on lower body **back** seam allowance. Stitch. Stuff head and body. Turn under body front seam allowance and hand stitch closed.

2. DRESS

   a. BODICE: Slit marked bodice piece at center to make 2 back bodice pieces. Stitch front and back bodice pieces together at shoulders, right sides together.

   b. HEM BODICE: Stitch narrow hem (⅛″) at center back and neck edges.

   c. SLEEVES: Stitch 2 rows of gathering threads, ⅛″ and ¼″ from edge, along one side of each sleeve. Pin centers of sleeves to shoulder seams. Gather sleeves to fit armholes and stitch. Press seam allowances toward bodice.

1″ Grid for Making Pattern Pieces

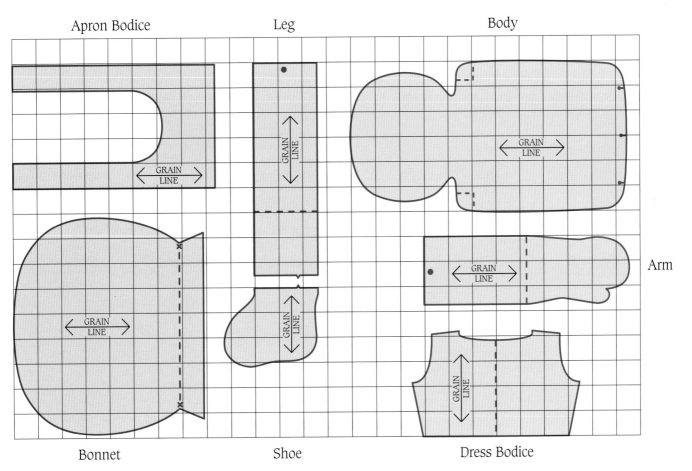

Apron Bodice   Leg   Body

GRAIN LINE

GRAIN LINE

GRAIN LINE

Arm

GRAIN LINE

GRAIN LINE

GRAIN LINE

GRAIN LINE

Bonnet   Shoe   Dress Bodice

d. SIDE SEAMS: Right sides together and underarm seams matching, stitch bodice side and sleeve seams as one continuous seam.

e. HEM SLEEVES: Stitch narrow hem at bottom edge of each sleeve.

f. SKIRT: Stitch 2 rows of gathering threads, ⅛″ and ¼″ from edge, along one long edge of skirt rectangle. Divide edge into quarters and mark with pins. Place skirt and bodice right sides together, matching pins to center front, center back, and side seams of bodice. Gather to fit. Stitch. Press seam toward bodice. Stitch center back seam of skirt.

g. SKIRT HEM: Press ¼″ then 1½″ to wrong side on bottom edge of skirt. Stitch.

h. FINISH: Place dress on doll. Make 2 pleats in lower edge of each sleeve and tack in place. Tack back neck opening closed. Use powder blush or colored pencil to color doll's cheeks.

3. PANTALOONS

a. SEAMS: Place rectangles right sides together. Mark inner leg seam placement. See diagram. Stitch side seams and ¼″ away from inner leg line, on both sides, as shown. Cut on marked line. Turn right side out and press.

b. HEMS: Stitch narrow hems at bottom edges of legs and waist.

c. GATHER: With six-strand embroidery floss and a blunt needle, using narrow hems as casings, gather waist and legs. Pull floss through, leaving long ends.

d. FINISH: Place pantaloons on doll. Pull up floss to fit waist and ankles. Tie in knots, then in bows.

Continued on page 78

2a.

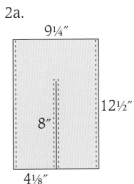

9¼″

12½″

8″

4⅛″

77

4. APRON

a. BODICE: Stitch bodice pieces, right sides together, leaving bottom edge open. Clip curves and trim corners. Turn right side out. Press.

b. SKIRT: Stitch narrow hems on both 7¼″ edges and one 10½″ edge of apron skirt. Stitch 2 rows of gathering threads, ⅛″ and ¼″ from edge, along remaining edge.

c. POCKET: Press ¼″ to wrong side on all 4 edges of pocket. Topstitch "hem" on one side. Pin pocket on apron skirt 2″ down and 2″ over from upper right edge. Stitch sides and bottom.

d. GATHER: Gather unhemmed edge of skirt to fit apron bodice. Pin raw edges of bodice to wrong side of skirt. Stitch. Seam will be on right side.

e. TIE: Press tie in half lengthwise, wrong sides together. Open out and press long edges ¼″ to wrong side. Mark center. Pin tie to cover skirt/bodice seam, matching centers. Beginning at one end, edge stitch open edges of tie, continuing across bodice/skirt to other end of tie. Edge stitch remaining edge of tie where it crosses bodice/skirt. Turn ends of shoulder straps under 1″, forming loops. Stitch ends of shoulder straps.

f. FINISH: Place apron on doll, pull waist ties through loops in ends of shoulder straps, and tie ends in a bow.

5. BONNET

a. BRIM: Iron interfacing to wrong sides of brim pieces. Stitch brim pieces right sides together on 2 short and 1 long edge. Trim corners and turn right side out. Press. Topstitch in 3 parallel lines ½″ apart measuring from long seamed edge.

b. BACK EDGE: Stitch bonnet pieces right sides together along straight edges between Xs. Clip to stitching at Xs. Turn. Press. Lightly mark dotted line on right side.

c. GATHER: Catching both pieces of fabric, stitch 2 rows of gathering threads, ⅛″ and ¼″ from edge, along curved edge of crown. Gather crown to fit brim. Stitch.

d. TIES: Cut two 12″ pieces of ribbon. Fold under ¼″ on one end of each and tack at Xs.

e. BACK EDGE: Using black embroidery floss, hand sew a running stitch along dotted line. Gather to 4″. Knot and clip thread.

f. FINISH: Place bonnet on doll and tie bow under chin.

Duckie Warmer

Photo on page 17. Pattern is on insert.

Fabric & Supplies

Polar fleece	yellow	2 squares 9″ - body
	orange	1 square 2″ - beak
Cotton print	yellow	¼ yd
Cotton print	blue	1 tiny scrap - eye
Velcro®		1 piece 2″
Buckwheat or rice		small amount
Fiberfil		small amount

Cutting

Polar fleece	yellow	1 body, 1 body reversed
	orange	1 beak
Cotton print	yellow	1 body reversed
		1 wing
		2 pieces 2½ x 4½″
Cotton print	blue	1 eye

Directions

Use ¼″ seam allowance.

1. DUCKY

    a. Applique wing and eye to body front.

    b. Trim 1″ from bottom edge of pocket piece. Stitch a narrow double hem on trimmed edge.

    c. Stitch Velcro® piece to center of hemmed edge on wrong side. Pin pocket piece wrong side down on right side of back body piece to determine placement for other side of Velcro®. Mark placement, unpin pieces, and stitch Velcro® in place.

    d. Pin or baste pocket to body back, wrong side of pocket to right side of body back. Pin or baste body front to body back/pocket, wrong sides together, sandwiching beak between fleece layers. Stitch ¼″ from edge using a narrow open zigzag, leaving 2-3″ open on bottom edge for stuffing. Stuff lightly with fiberfill. Stitch opening closed.

2. BUCKWHEAT PACKET: Place 2½ x 4½″ pieces right sides together and stitch all around outside edge, leaving small opening on one side for filling. Turn right side out and fill with buckwheat. Stitch opening closed.

3. USE: Heat buckwheat packet in microwave briefly, until warm. Place packet in ducky. Use ducky to warm and comfort your baby.

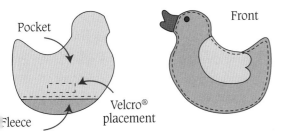

1d.

Back

Pocket

Front

Velcro® placement

Fleece

Lambie Hot/Cold Pack Cover

Photo on page 31
Pattern is on insert. See additional directions there.

Fabric & Supplies

Sherpa fleece		3 pieces 9 x 13″ - body
Cotton flannel	brown	⅛ yd - legs
	plaid	⅙ yd - bow
Applique	pink, black	⅛ yd each
Velcro®		1 piece 8″
Hot/cold pack		4 x 9″ reusable gel-type
Fiberfill		small amount

Cutting

Sherpa		1 body piece for front
Cotton flannel	brown	8 legs - see insert
	plaid	1 piece 4½ x 21″ - bow
Applique		1 set - face & inner part of ears

Directions   Use ¼″ seam allowance.

1. LAMBIE

    a. Applique face and ears to body front. Place 2 leg pieces right sides together and stitch all but top edge. Turn and stuff lightly. Make 4.

    b. Trim 2½″ from one long edge of pocket rectangle. Stitch a narrow single hem on trimmed edge. Stitch Velcro® to hemmed edge on wrong side, centered. Pin pocket piece wrong side down on right side of back body rectangle, raw edges even, to determine placement for other side of Velcro®. Mark, unpin, and stitch Velcro® in place.

    c. Pin or baste pocket piece to body back piece, wrong side of pocket to right side of body back. Pin or baste body front to body back/pocket, wrong sides together, sandwiching legs between front and back pieces. Stitch ¼″ from body front edge, leaving 3″ open on top edge for stuffing. Trim pocket and back pieces even with front. Stuff lightly. Stitch opening closed.

2. BOW: Fold bow piece lengthwise, right sides together, and stitch all around outside edge, leaving 3″ open for turning. Trim corners, turn right side out, and press. Stitch opening closed. Tie into a bow and tack to lambie's head.

3. USE: Heat or chill gel pack using manufacturer's directions. Place packet in lambie. Use lambie to comfort your baby.

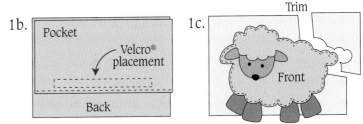

1b.

Pocket

Velcro® placement

Back

1c.

Trim

Front

FAVORITE QUILTS FAST & FUN

Complete yardage/cutting charts for 7 old favorites in 5 sizes each for both Basic and Scrap versions. Extra-large diagrams.

FRIENDS FOREVER QUILTING TOGETHER

A unique quilting book with ideas for gifts for friends, block & fabric exchange quilts, & more. Over 28 projects.

HEARTS APLENTY

Need a gift for a loved one? This collection of 19 quilts and small projects is perfect. A variety of techniques, styles, and skill levels.

DIVIDE & CONQUER

Divide a bed-sized quilt into workable sections & Conquer the task of machine or hand quilting it. Four great methods. 17 original quilts.

FIVE EASY PIECES

Use beautiful large florals to make custom decorator-style quilts and accessories. Large blocks and applique shapes make the quilts quick!

HOME FOR THE HARVEST

Celebrate autumn with 18 quilts & more than 20 small projects. Back-to-school, Halloween, & Thanksgiving themes.

BEDWARMERS

Wrap your comforter in patchwork with one of three styles of comforter covers. Plus coordinated toppers, pillow covers, & pillowcases.

JOY TO THE WORLD

Full of holiday quilts for different skill levels, this popular book contains delightful projects—gift bags, stockings, tree skirts, and place mats.

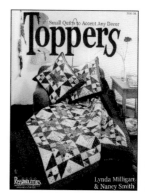

TOPPERS

Toppers are beautiful quilts for displaying over bed pillows, on the back of a couch, or over a comforter or bedspread. A variety of styles.

QUILTS & MORE

Over 25 projects using photos transferred to fabric. Instructions & full-sized patterns for making special family heirlooms.

HOUSEWARMERS

Warm your home with the beauty of homemade quilts. Add personal touches to any room. Nineteen quilts & 25 smaller projects.

TIME FOR A CHAIN

Detailed charts for rotary cutting give measurements for single, double, and triple Irish Chains in two or three block sizes each.

P.S. I LOVE YOU TWO!

One of our national top sellers featuring timeless projects for making cherished gifts for babies and children. A multitude of techniques.

POSSIBILITIES®

...Fabric Designers for AvLyn, Inc., publishers of DreamSpinners® patterns & I'll Teach Myself™ & Possibilities® books...

Home of Great American Quilt Factory, Inc.

These books are available from your local quilt shop or from Possibilities® at:

8970 East Hampden Avenue
Denver, Colorado 80231

Phone 303-740-6206 • Fax 303-220-7424
Orders only U.S. & Canada 1-800-474-2665
Order online at www.possibilitiesquilt.com